THE
NEW YORKER
BOOK OF LITERARY CARTOONS

THE
NEW YORKER
BOOK OF LITERARY CARTOONS

EDITED BY BOB MANKOFF

POCKET BOOKS
New York   London   Toronto   Sydney   Singapore

This book is a work of fiction. Names, characters, places and incidents are products of the author's imagination or are used fictitiously. Any resemblance to actual events or locales or persons living or dead is entirely coincidental.

 POCKET BOOKS, a division of Simon & Schuster, Inc.
1230 Avenue of the Americas, New York, NY 10020

ISBN: 0-671-03557-6

First Pocket Books hardcover printing September 2000

10 9 8 7 6 5 4 3 2 1

POCKET and colophon are registered trademarks of Simon & Schuster, Inc.

Book design by Lindgren/Fuller Design

Printed in the U. S. A.

THE
NEW YORKER
BOOK OF LITERARY CARTOONS

"What the hell ever happened to the old-fashioned love story?"

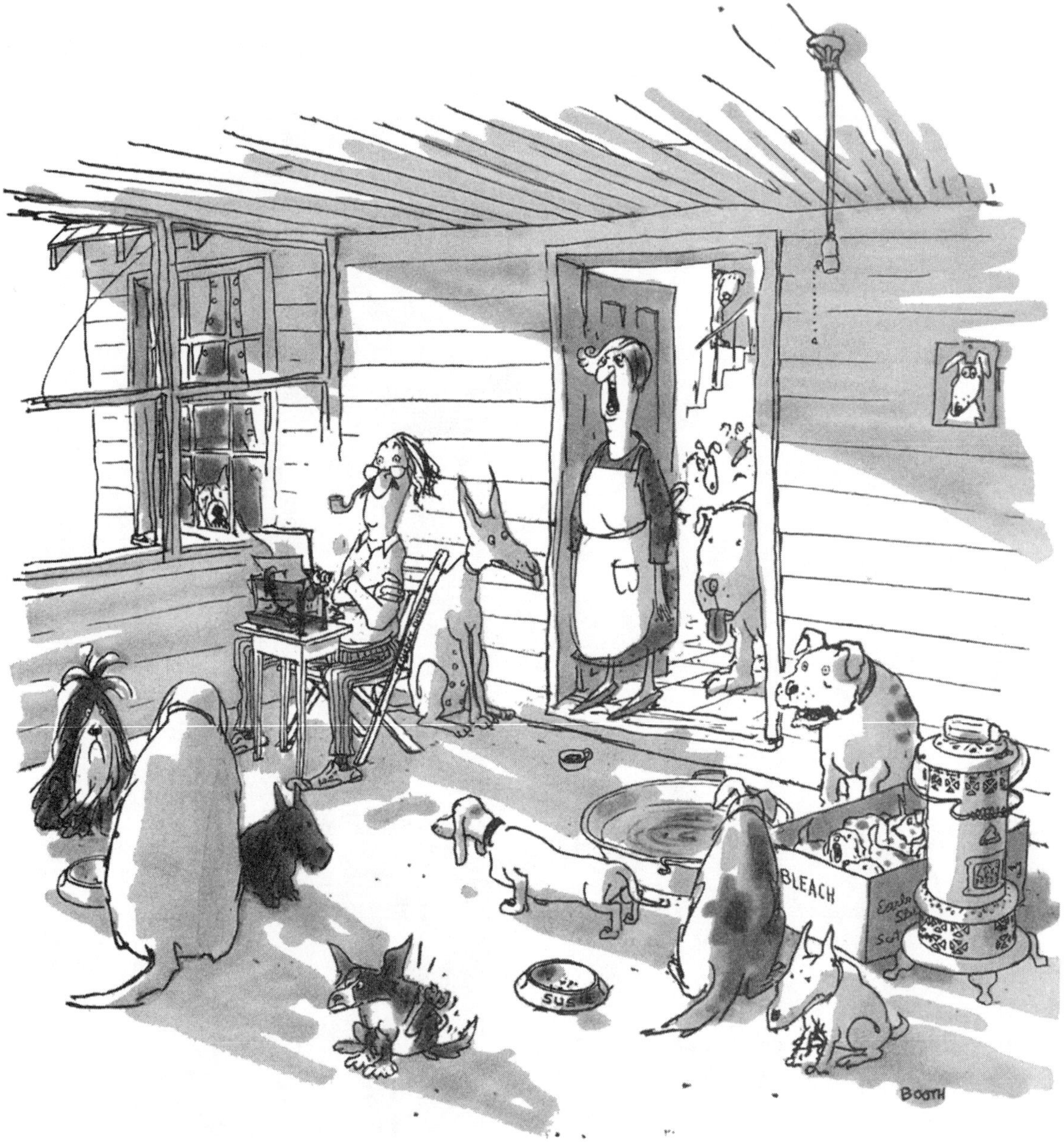
BLEACH
SUSIE
BOOTH

"Write about dogs!"

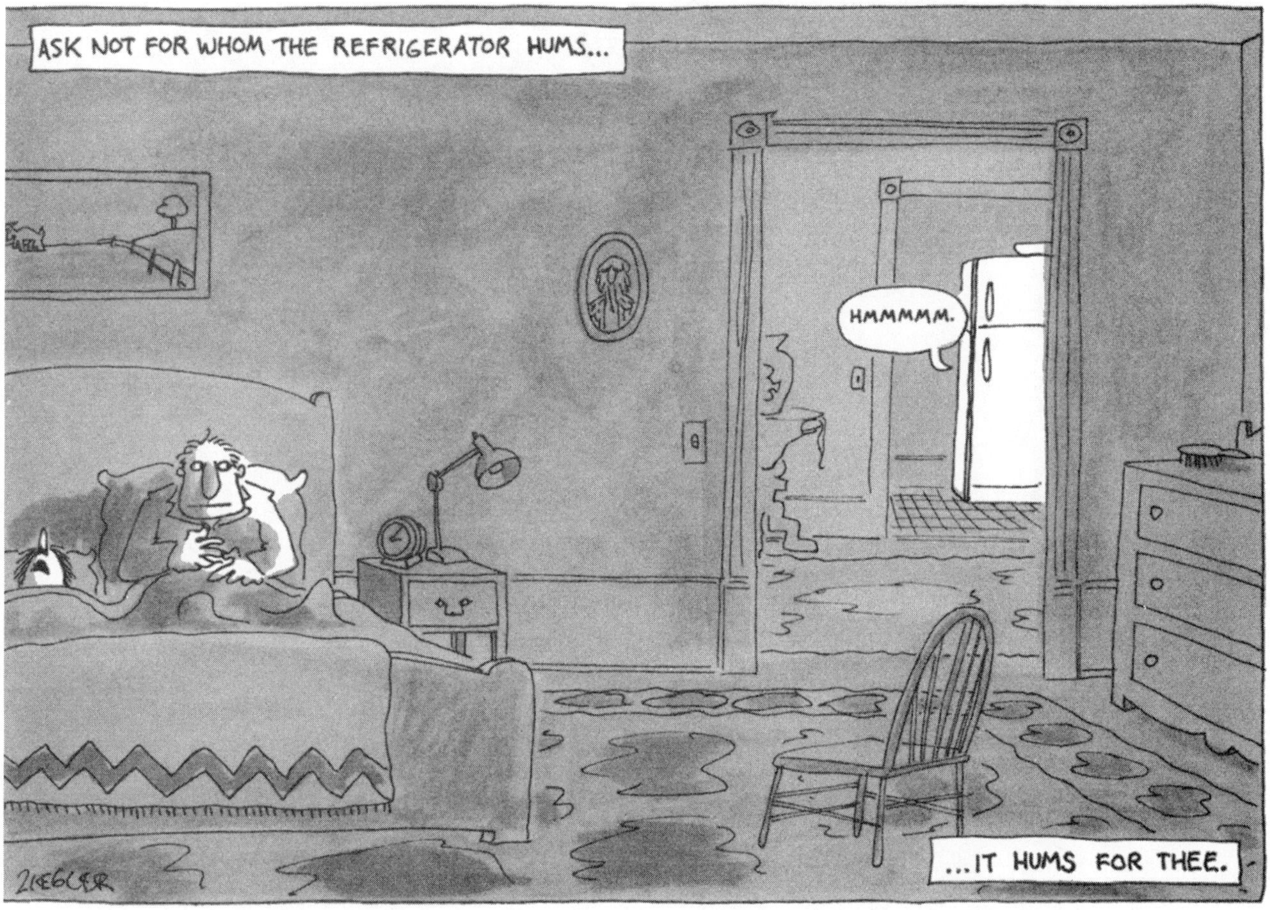
ASK NOT FOR WHOM THE REFRIGERATOR HUMS...
HMMMMM.
...IT HUMS FOR THEE.
ZIEGLER

"If you were to boil your book down to a few words, what would be its message?"

"It's a bedtime story. It doesn't _need_ corroboration."

5

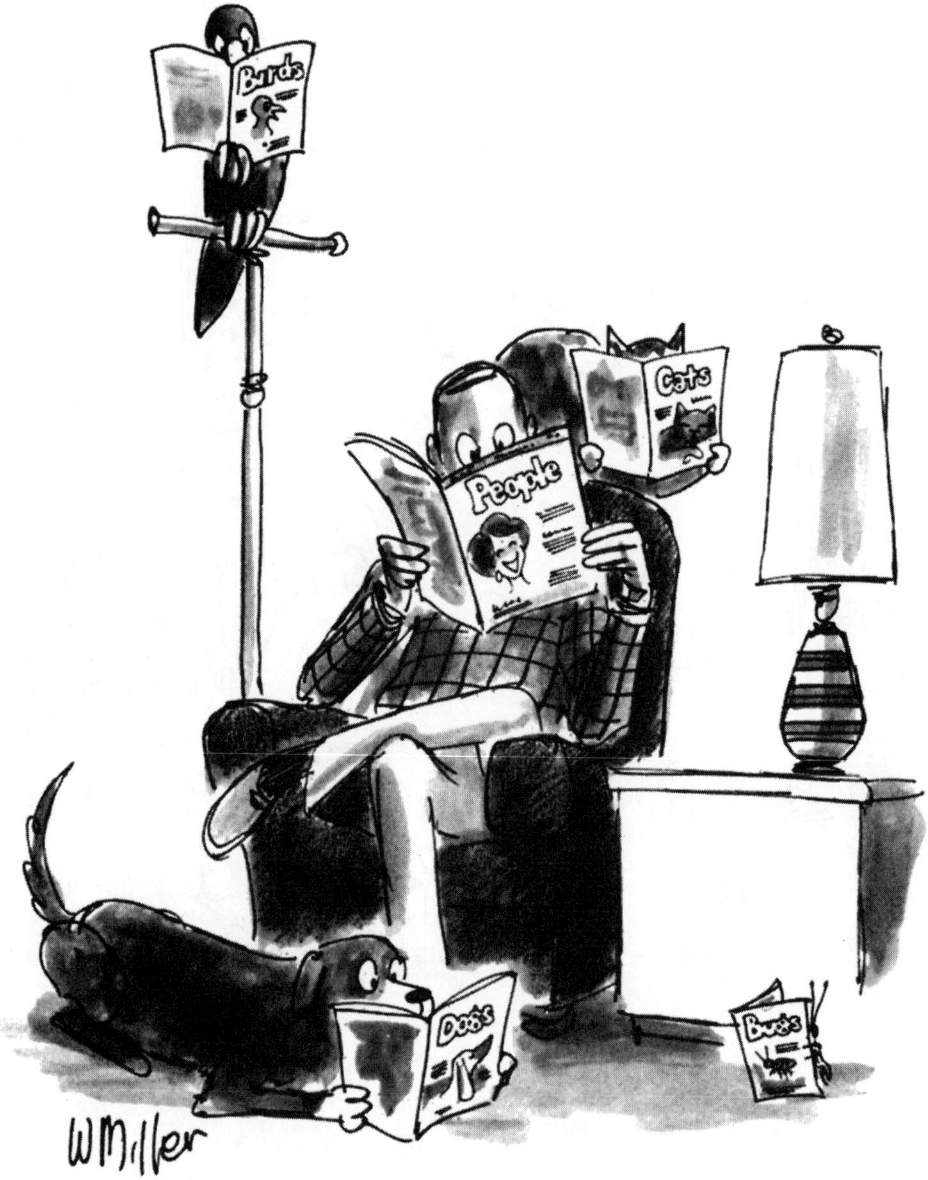
Birds
People
Cats
Dogs
Bugs
W Miller

"I'm afraid that novel in you will have to come out."

"I wish you would make up your mind, Mr. Dickens.
Was it the best of times or was it the worst of times?
It could scarcely have been both."

"Wait a minute. Where am I going? I'm a writer."

9

IT'S THE MIRACLE BOOK!

EVERYTHING IN A NUTSHELL
by BETTY-ELLEN BELKNAP

- It will help you be a better you!
- You will lose 30 pounds in 30 days!
- You will buy real estate with no money down!
- You will win friends and influence people!
- Contains lots of gossip!
- Contains tons of historical facts!
- You will be able to closely identify with every single character!
- You will experience every emotion known to mankind!

YOU NEED NEVER BUY ANOTHER BOOK AGAIN FOR THE REST OF YOUR LIFE !!!

R. Chast

"Hey! Just wanted to say I <u>loved</u> the Book of Kells."

"I do want to solve all my problems, but I'll wait till it comes out in soft cover."

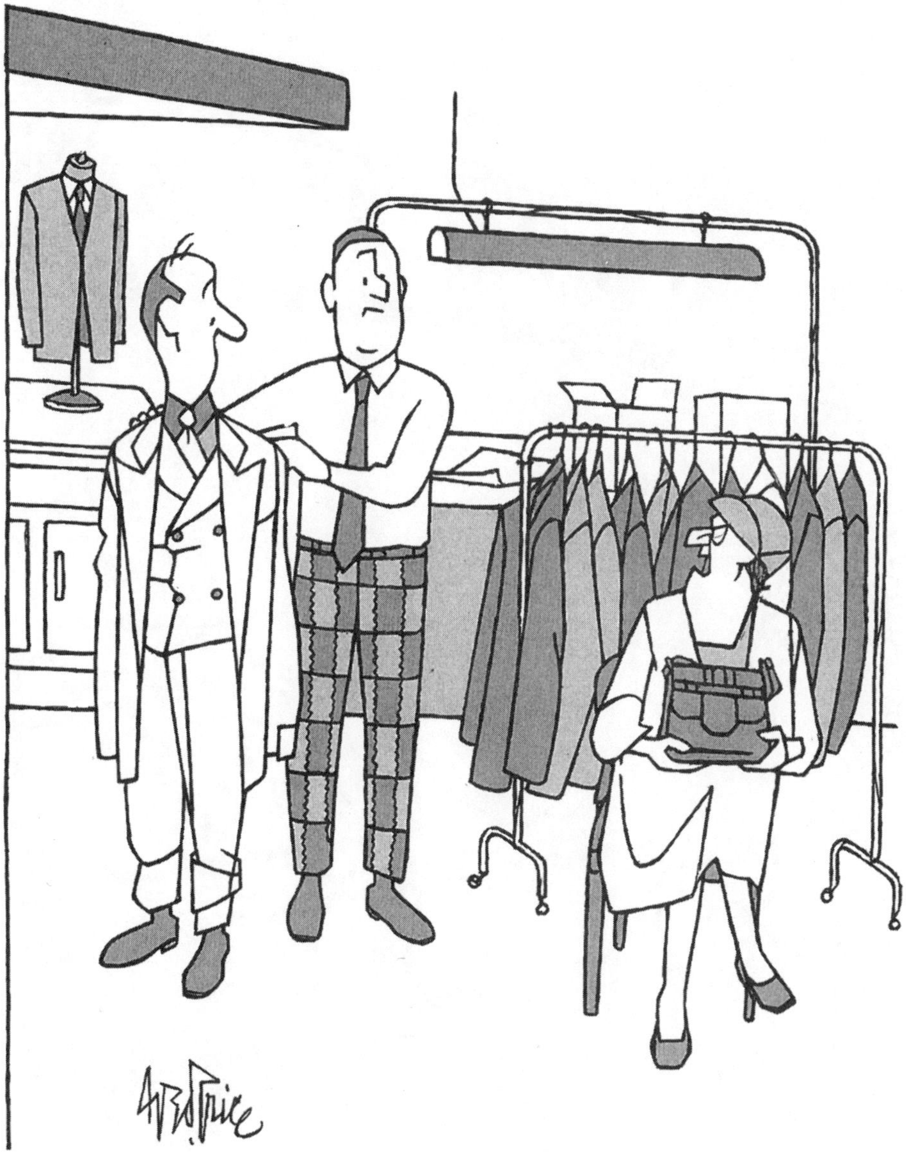
Alfred Price

"Too Tom Wolfeish!"

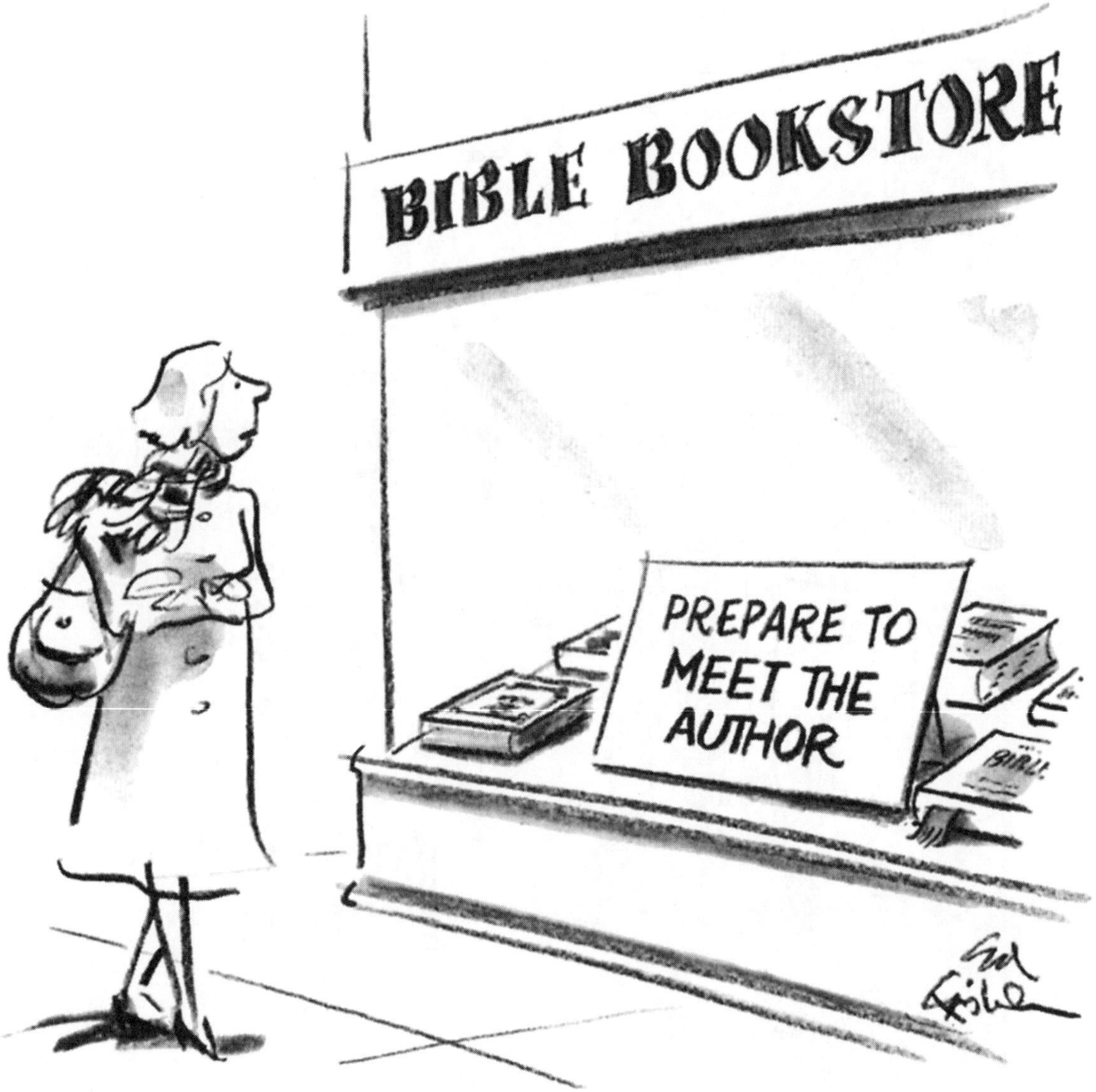
BIBLE BOOKSTORE
PREPARE TO MEET THE AUTHOR

"GONE WITH THE WIND": THE BEACH BLANKET

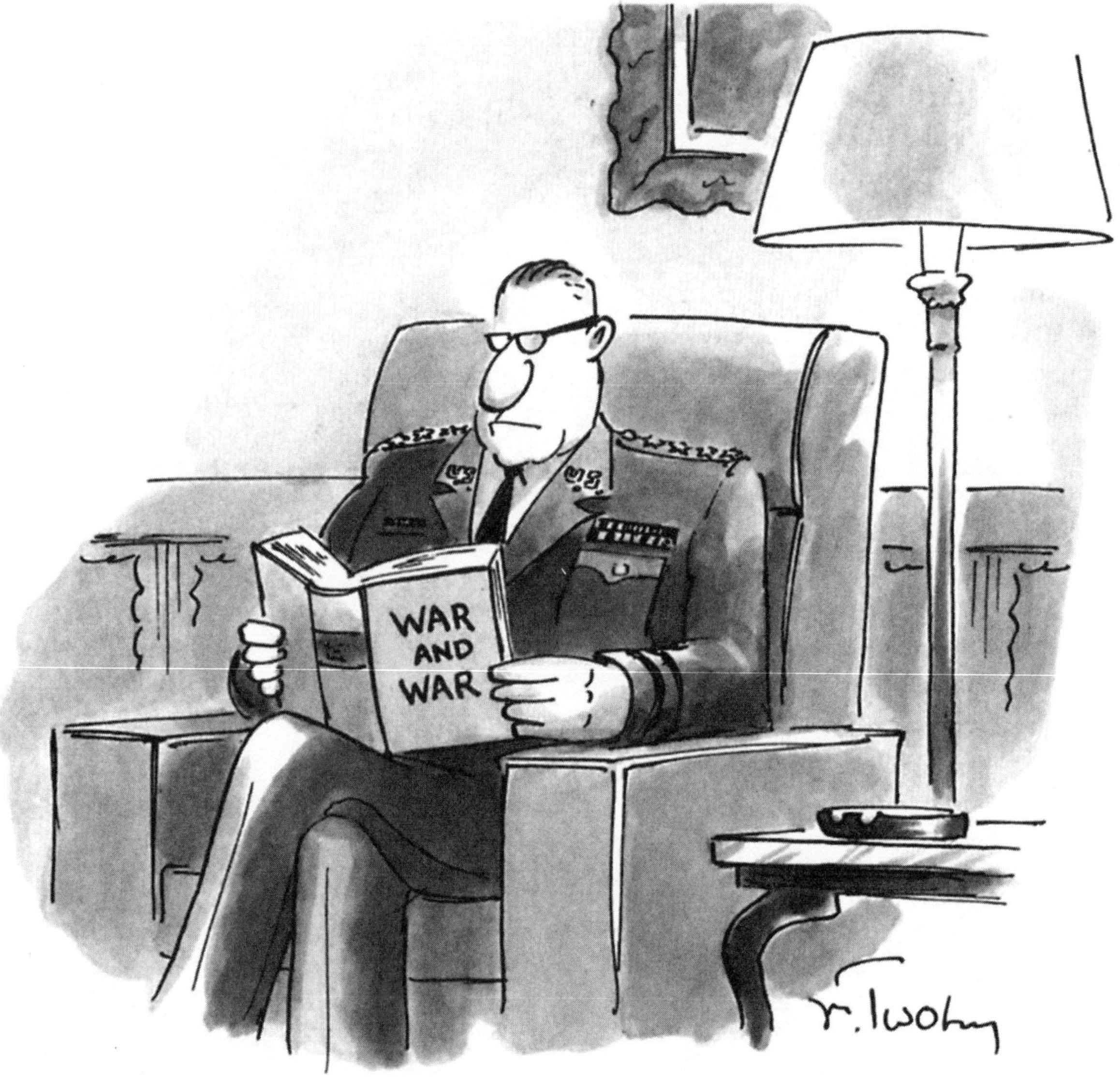
WAR
AND
WAR
r. Twohy

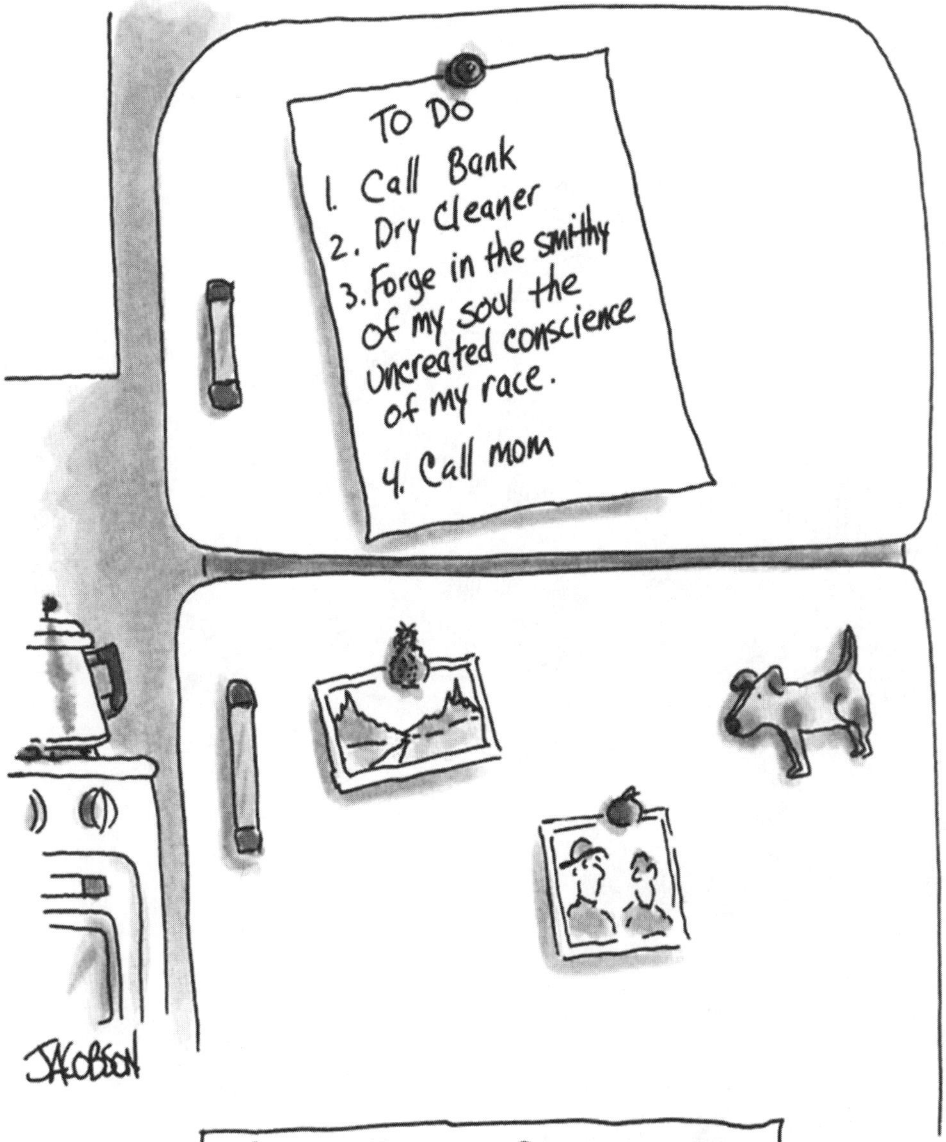
TO DO
1. Call Bank
2. Dry Cleaner
3. Forge in the smithy of my soul the uncreated conscience of my race.
4. Call mom
JACOBSON

JAMES JOYCE'S REFRIGERATOR

"Why, you're right. Tonight isn't reading night, tonight is sex night."

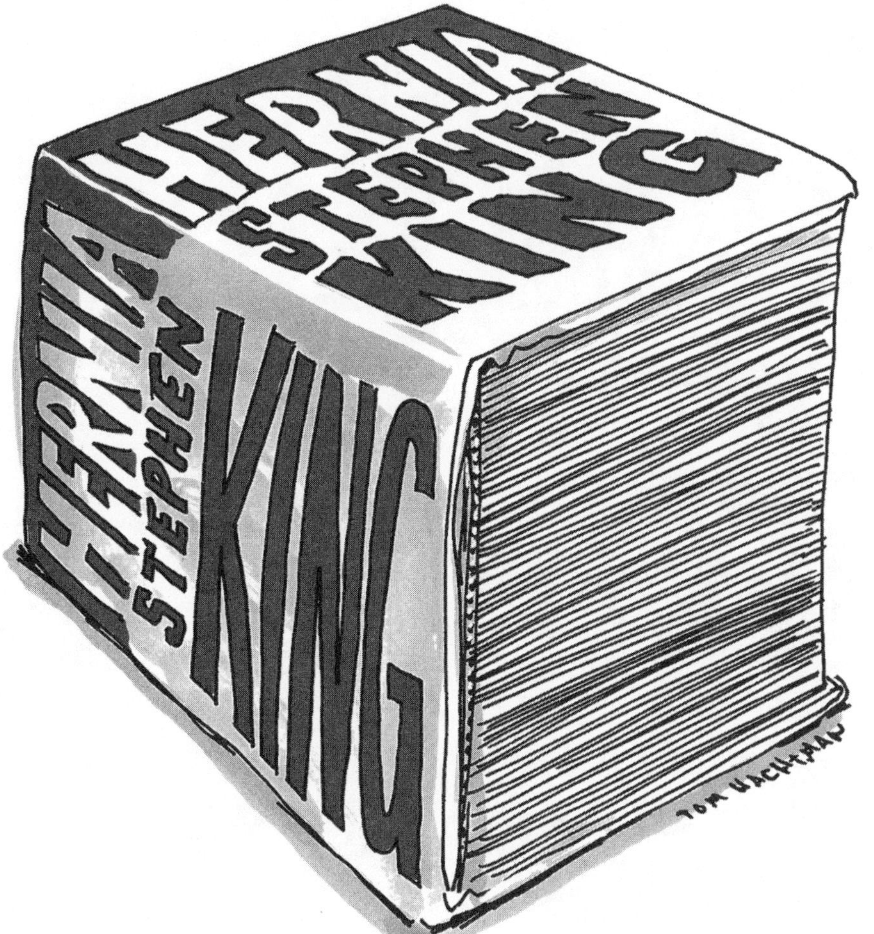
STEPHEN
KING
STEPHEN
KING
TOM HACHTMAN

"*Timothy, if you never watch TV you'll never know what's going on in the world.*"

"I don't have a title yet, or even a subject. All I have is
the price: twenty-three ninety-five in hardcover."

"Nevermore. And you can quote me."

"Can you believe it? A couple of page-turners,
one affair, and, wham—it's Labor Day."

"As a cost-cutting measure, for our fall list we
have decided to bypass traditional bookstore sales and subsequent
remaindering, and instead go directly to the shredder."

"Lately, I've been reading Jane Austen—just to clear my palate."

"Good, but not immortal."

"Oh, just hanging out, reading the Upanishads."

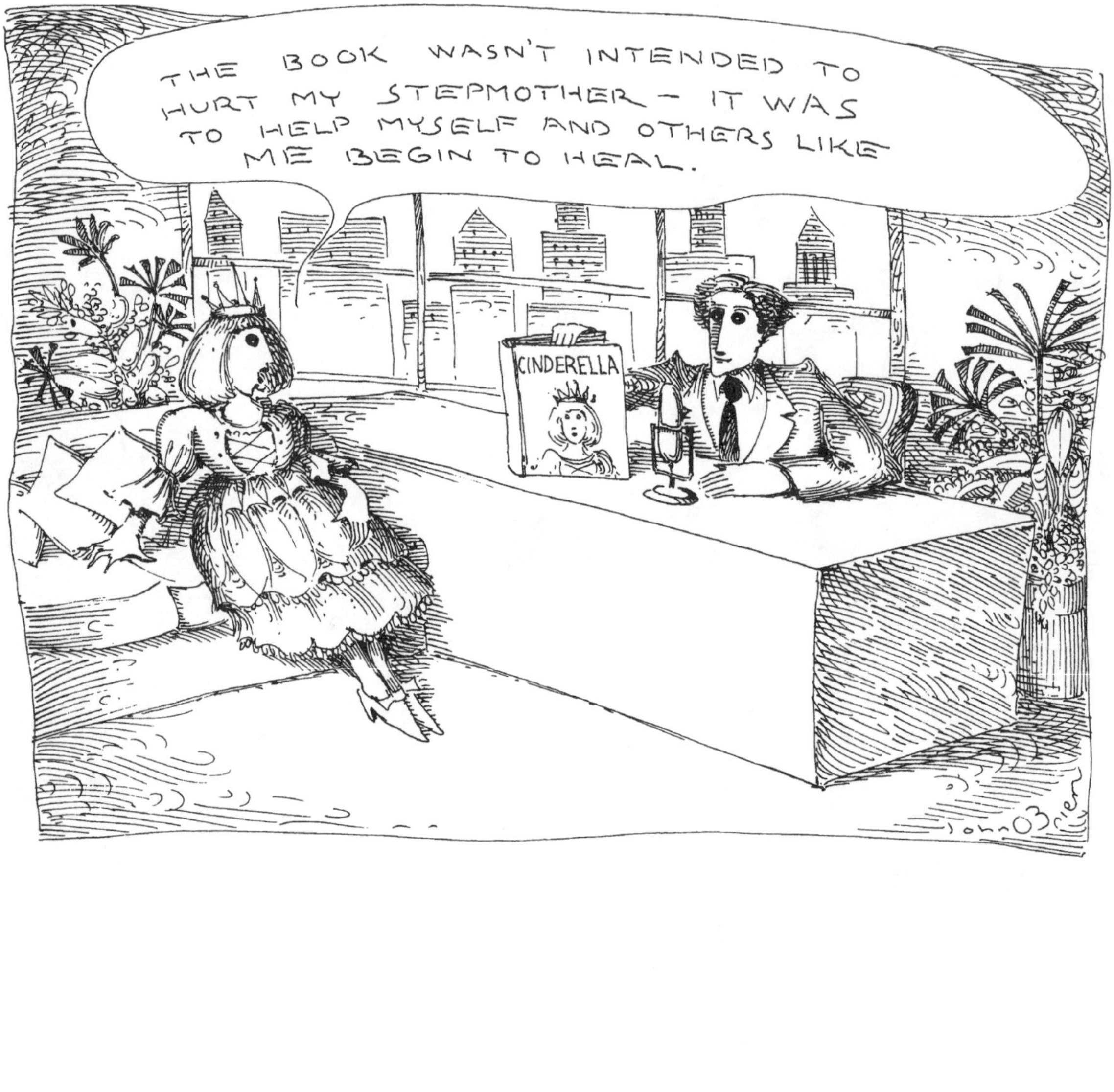
THE BOOK WASN'T INTENDED TO HURT MY STEPMOTHER – IT WAS TO HELP MYSELF AND OTHERS LIKE ME BEGIN TO HEAL.
CINDERELLA
John O'Brien

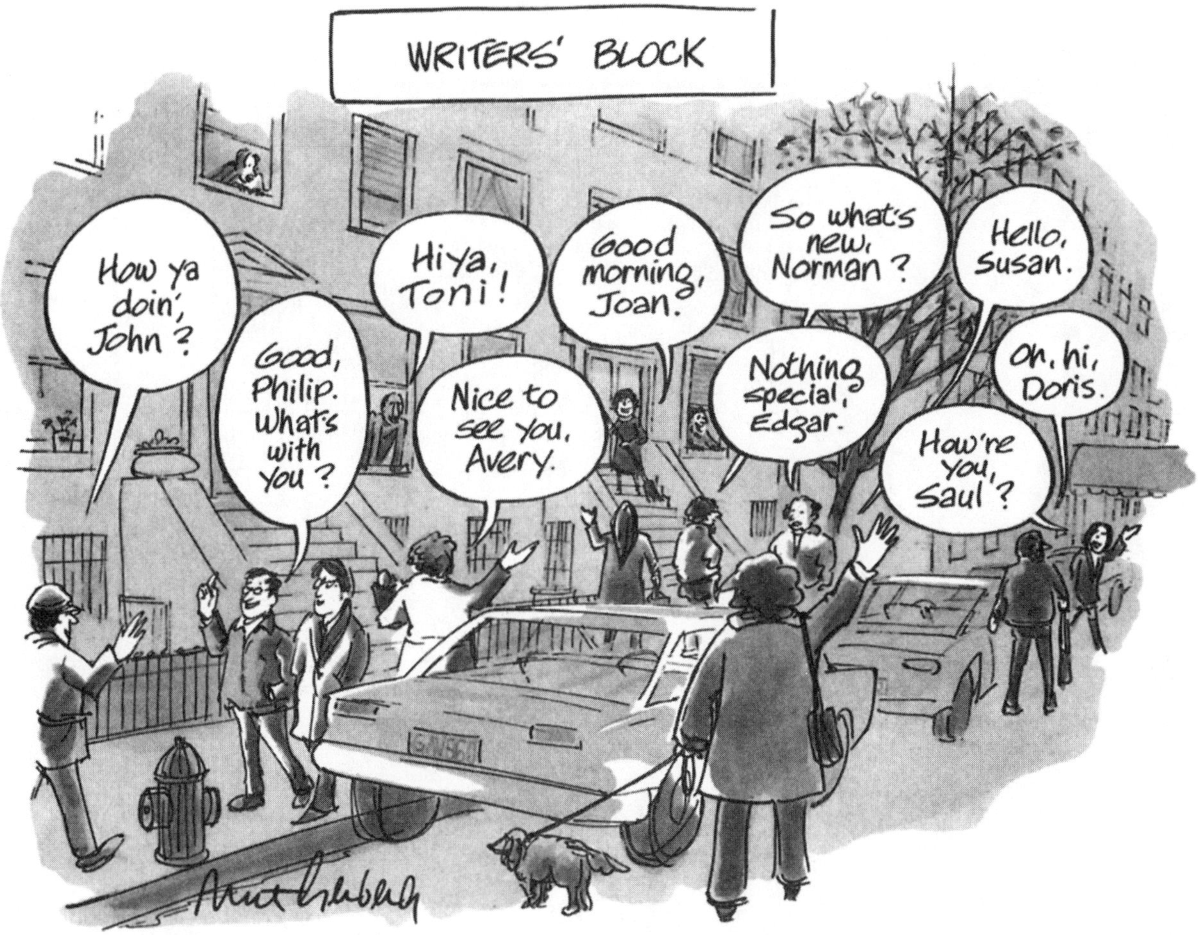
WRITERS' BLOCK
How ya doin', John?
Good, Philip. What's with you?
Hiya, Toni!
Nice to see you, Avery.
Good morning, Joan.
So what's new, Norman?
Nothing special, Edgar.
Hello, Susan.
Oh, hi, Doris.
How're you, Saul?

"WITH FIRST NOVELS I TEND TO FAVOR THIS APPROACH," EXPLAINED THE SENIOR EDITOR.

THE LETTERS OF JEAN-PAUL SARTRE TO HIS MOTHER

"You know, it's a picture book. Needless to say, it doesn't have a lot of narrative scope."

"I've got an idea for a story: Gus and Ethel live on Long Island, on the North Shore.
He works sixteen hours a day writing fiction. Ethel never goes out, never does anything except fix
Gus sandwiches and in the end she becomes a nympho-lesbo-killer-whore. Here's your sandwich."

"Read the book!" "See the movie!"

"Ignore him. He's the guy who's writing that unauthorized biography of me."

35

"Your editor wants to know if you have
enough flexibility to just give up."

REVISED TEXTS

Madame Bovary, Tennis Ace

Madame Bovary's mischief-creating boredom becomes a thing of the past when she discovers tennis.

The Great and Physically Fit Gatsby

The mystery man of West Egg changes his life by taking up running.

Hamlet, Swimmer of Denmark

The melancholy Prince learns that he can rid himself of anxiety and tension by swimming a mile a day.

R. Chast

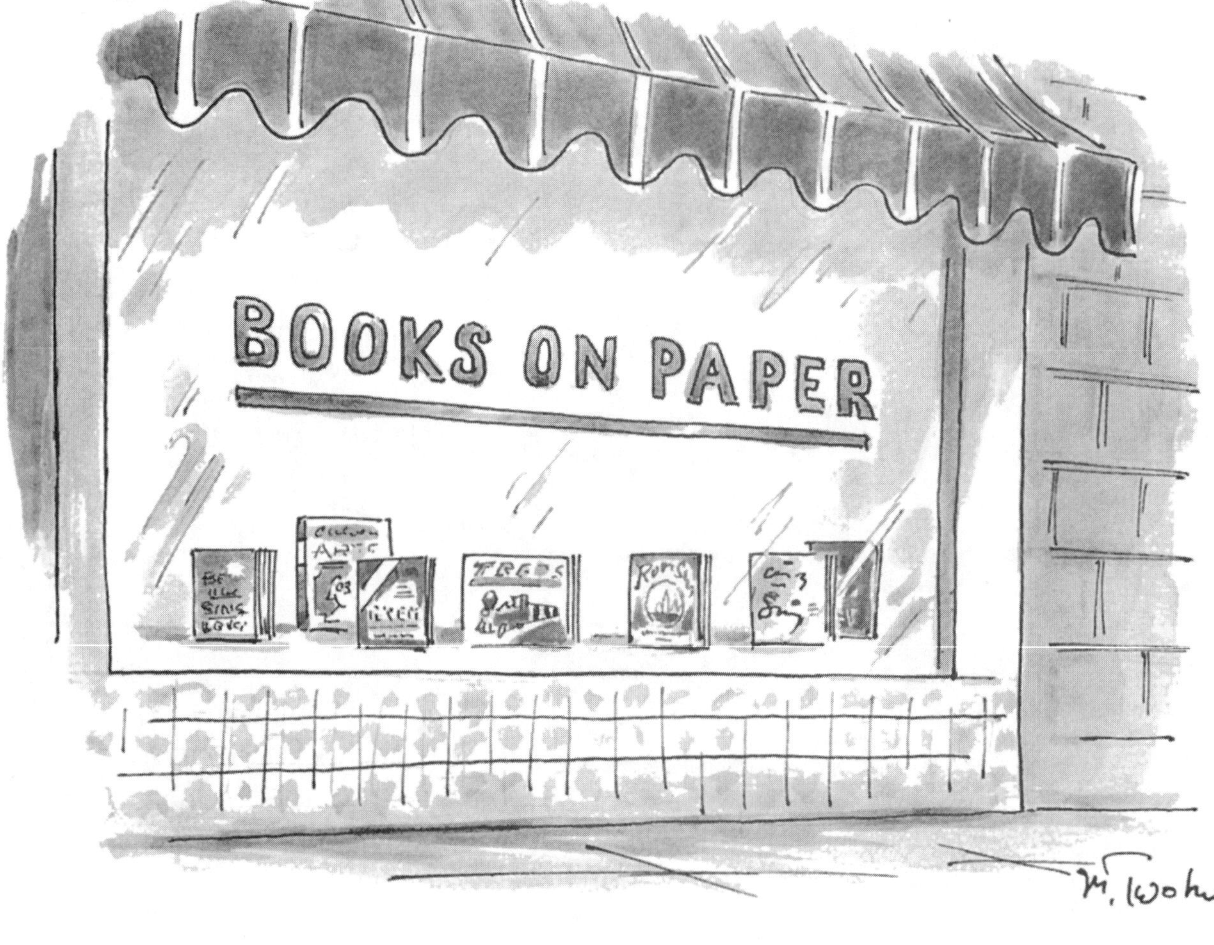
BOOKS ON PAPER

"I really, really enjoyed your hype."

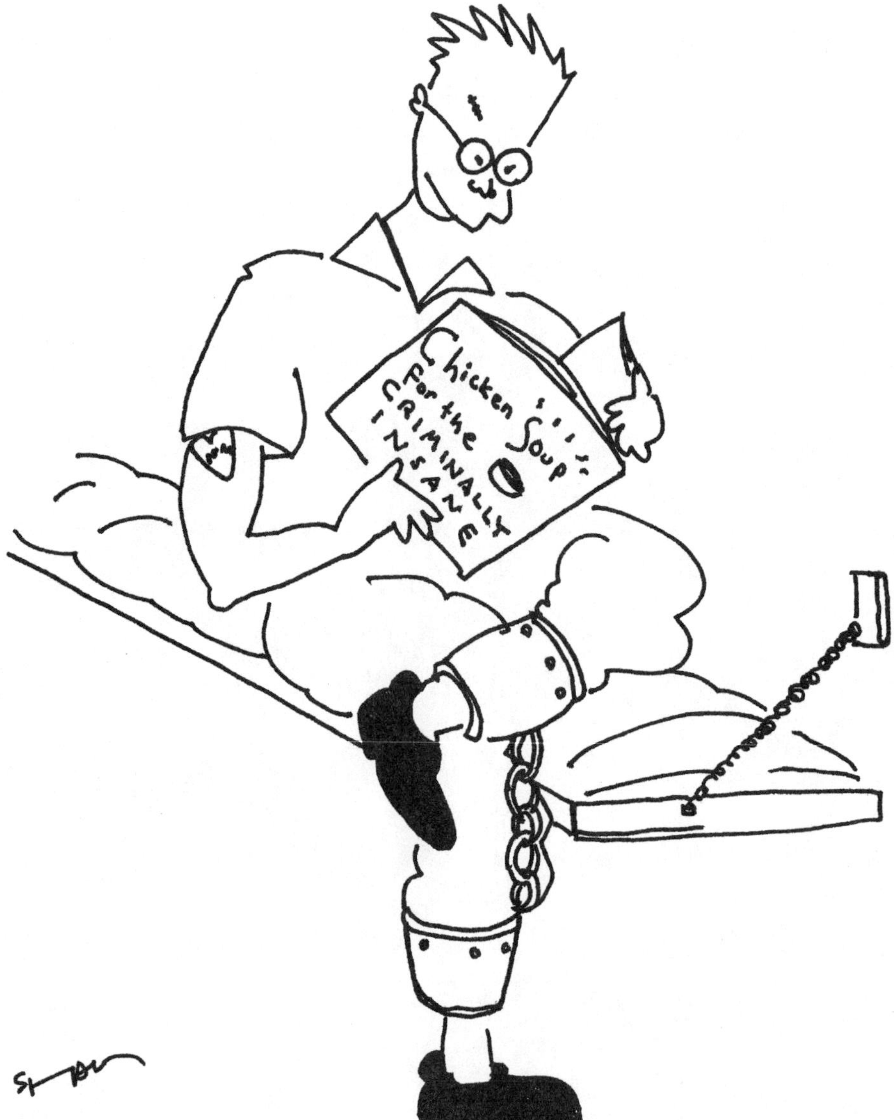
Chicken Soup for the CRIMINALLY INSANE

WHY THE DINOSAURS PERISHED

"Thank you for letting us consider the enclosed manuscript. Although it has obvious merit, we are sorry to say that it does not suit our present needs."

"Good evening. In today's top story, my book has jumped to Number Three on the best-seller list."

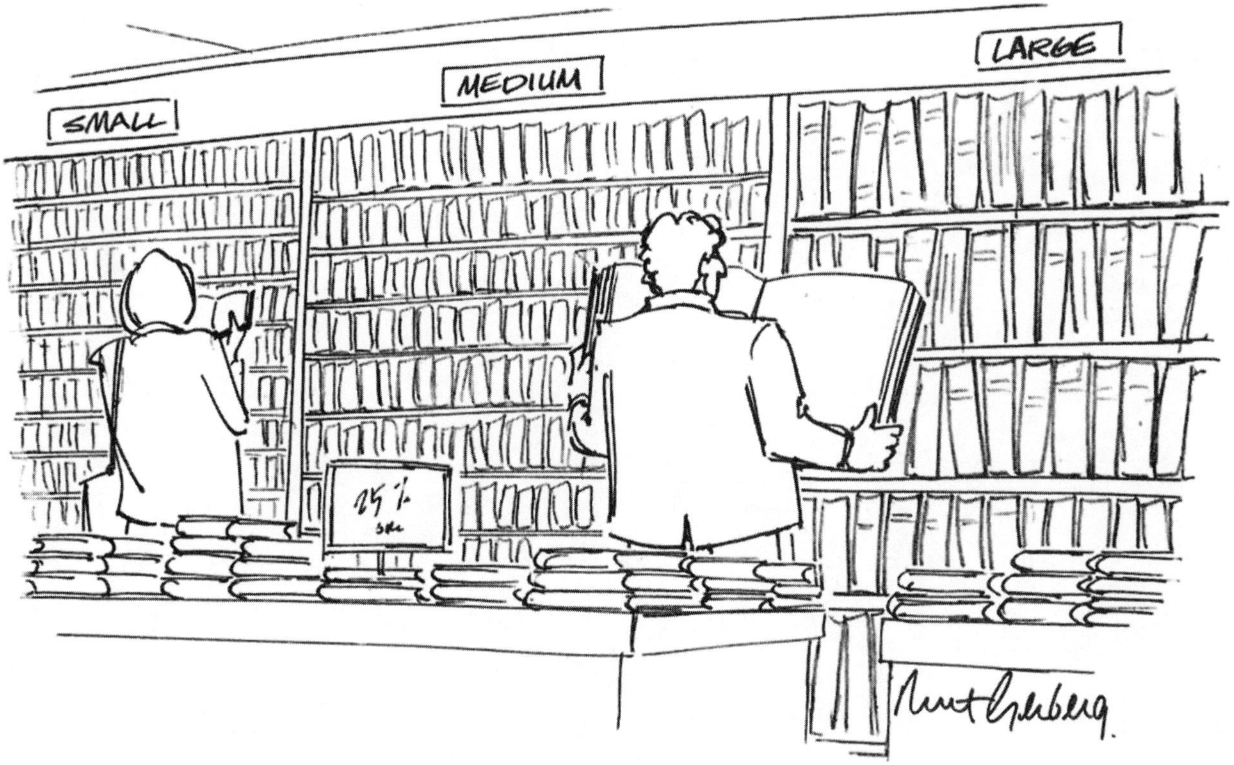
SMALL
MEDIUM
LARGE
25%

POSITIVE THOUGHT

AFFIRMATION THERAPY

SELF-HELPING

MORE JOY

EVERY DAY, EVERY WHICH WAY

CENTERING

MEDITATIONS

A NEW BEGINNING

FREE TO BE

MANKOFF

"Stop asking so many questions, or it's right back to Books on Tape for you."

"Hemingway! Is he any good?"

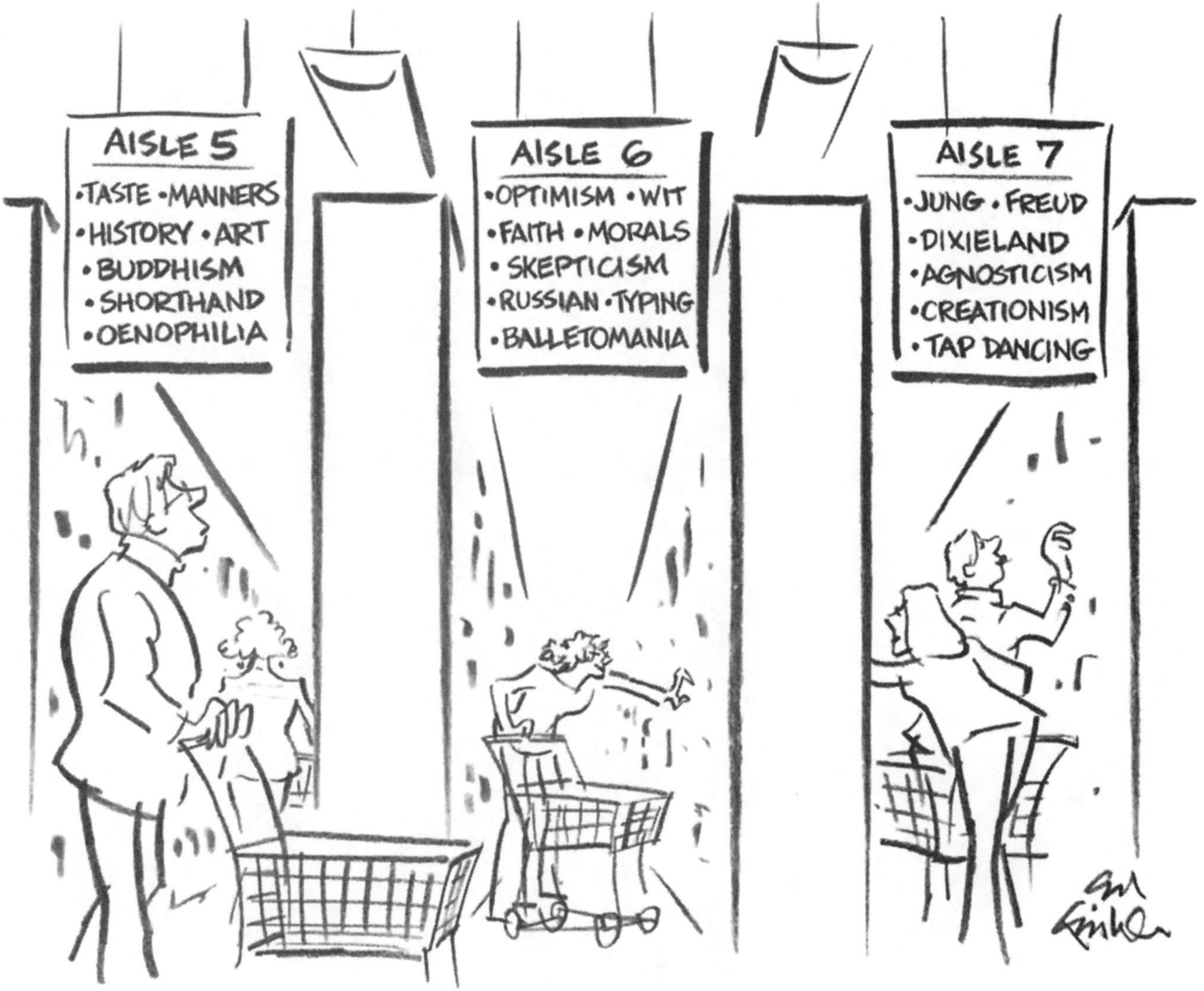
AISLE 5
•TASTE •MANNERS
•HISTORY •ART
•BUDDHISM
•SHORTHAND
•OENOPHILIA
AISLE 6
•OPTIMISM •WIT
•FAITH •MORALS
•SKEPTICISM
•RUSSIAN •TYPING
•BALLETOMANIA
AISLE 7
•JUNG •FREUD
•DIXIELAND
•AGNOSTICISM
•CREATIONISM
•TAP DANCING

THE GREAT CANADIAN NOVEL

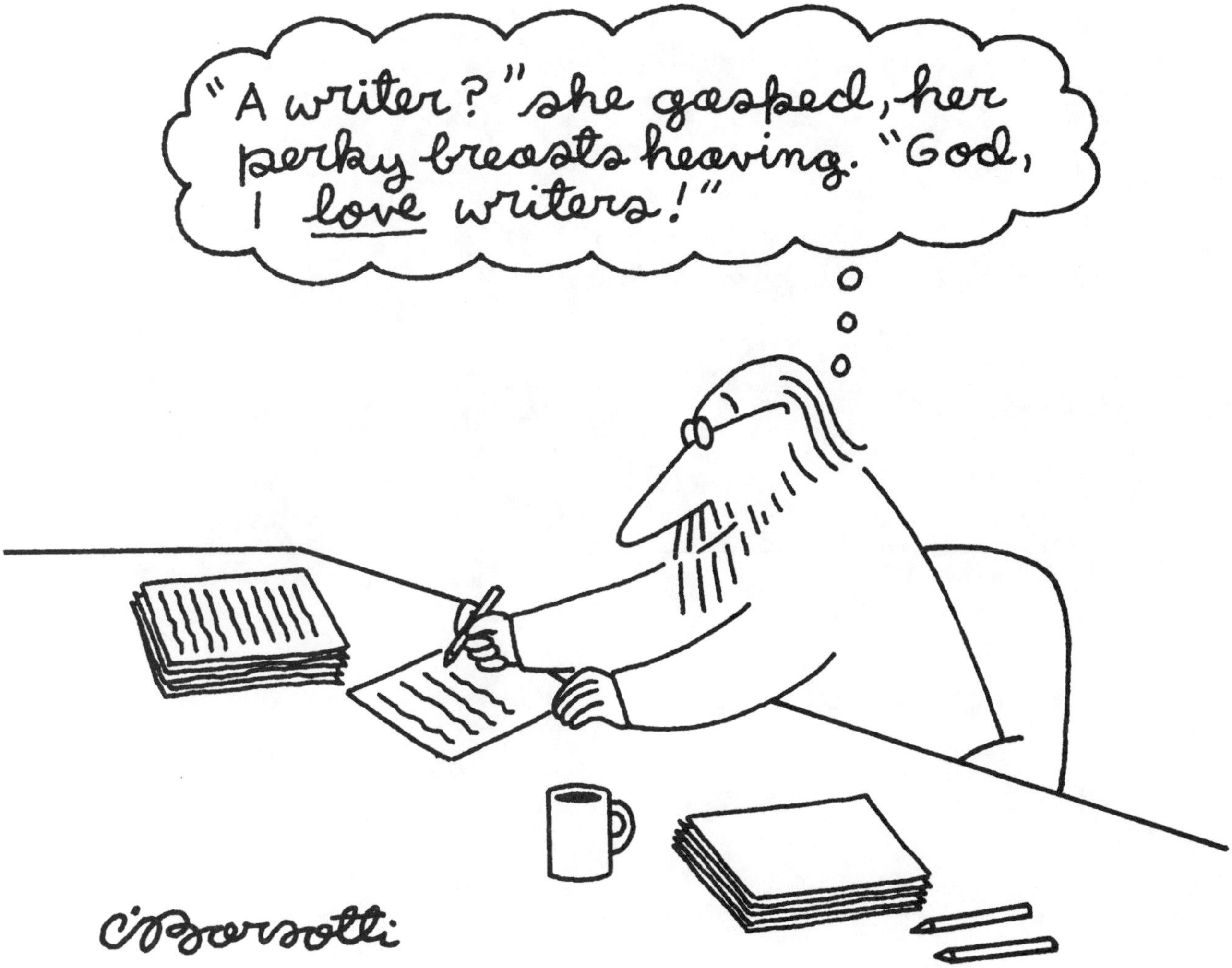
"A writer?" she gasped, her perky breasts heaving. "God, I love writers!"
C. Barsotti

"He leaves the new Sendak lying around, but he's never actually read it."

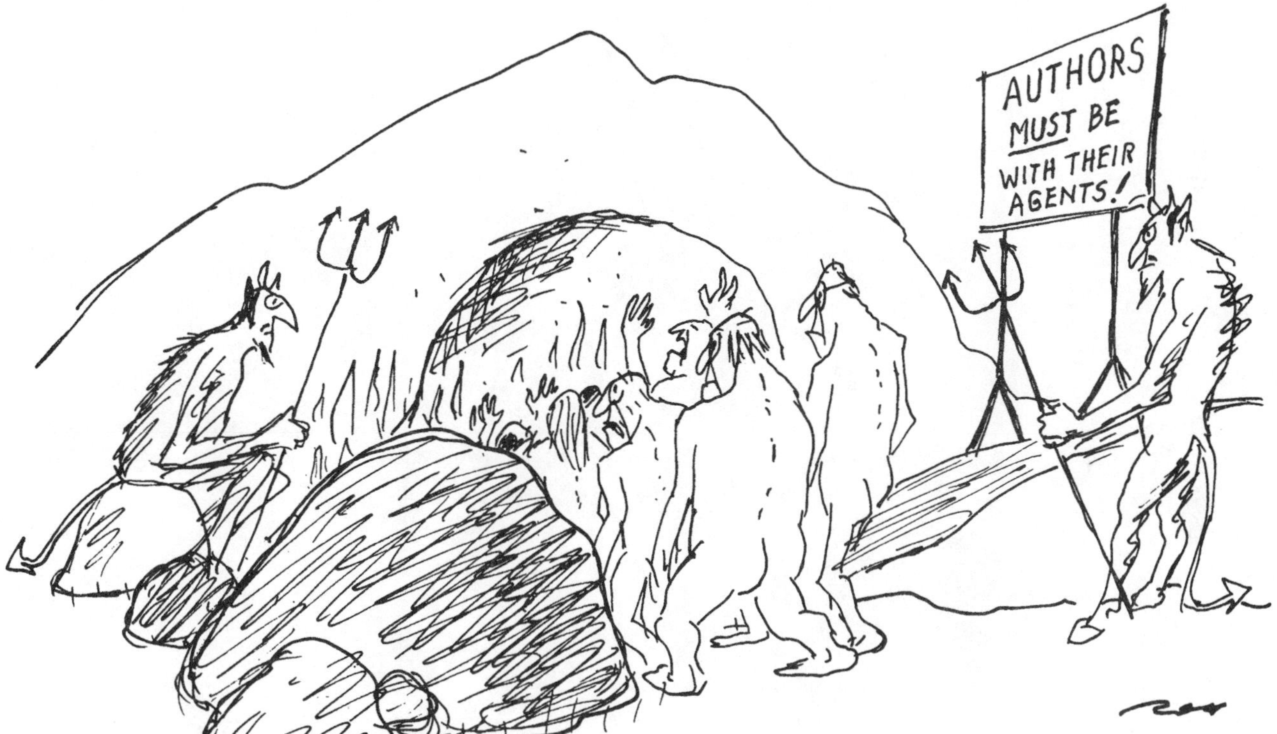
AUTHORS
MUST BE
WITH THEIR
AGENTS!

*"That is not one of the seven habits
of highly effective people."*

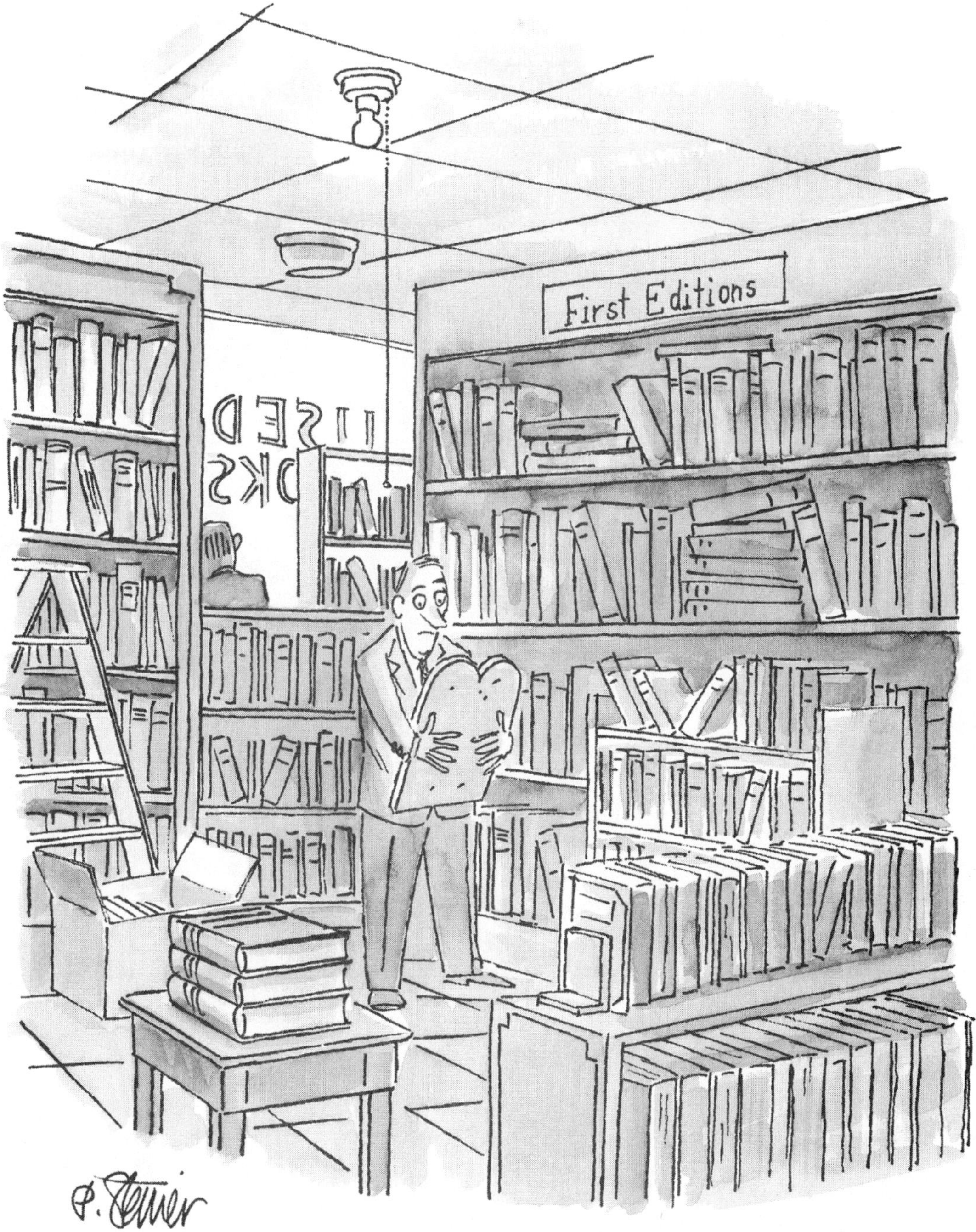
First Editions

"*Oprah is definite, Barnes and Noble is giving you front windows,
and Norman Mailer has agreed to a feud.*"

"I'm tired of people who write first novels."

"'How I Spent My Summer Vacation,' by Lilia Anya, all rights reserved, which includes the right to reproduce this essay or portions thereof in any form whatsoever, including, but not limited to, novel, screenplay, musical, television miniseries, home video, and interactive CD-ROM."

"Let me get you another copy. Someone left a slice of salami in this one."

*"She has the true Emily Dickinson spirit except
that she gets fed up occasionally."*

"I can't help thinking there's a book in this."

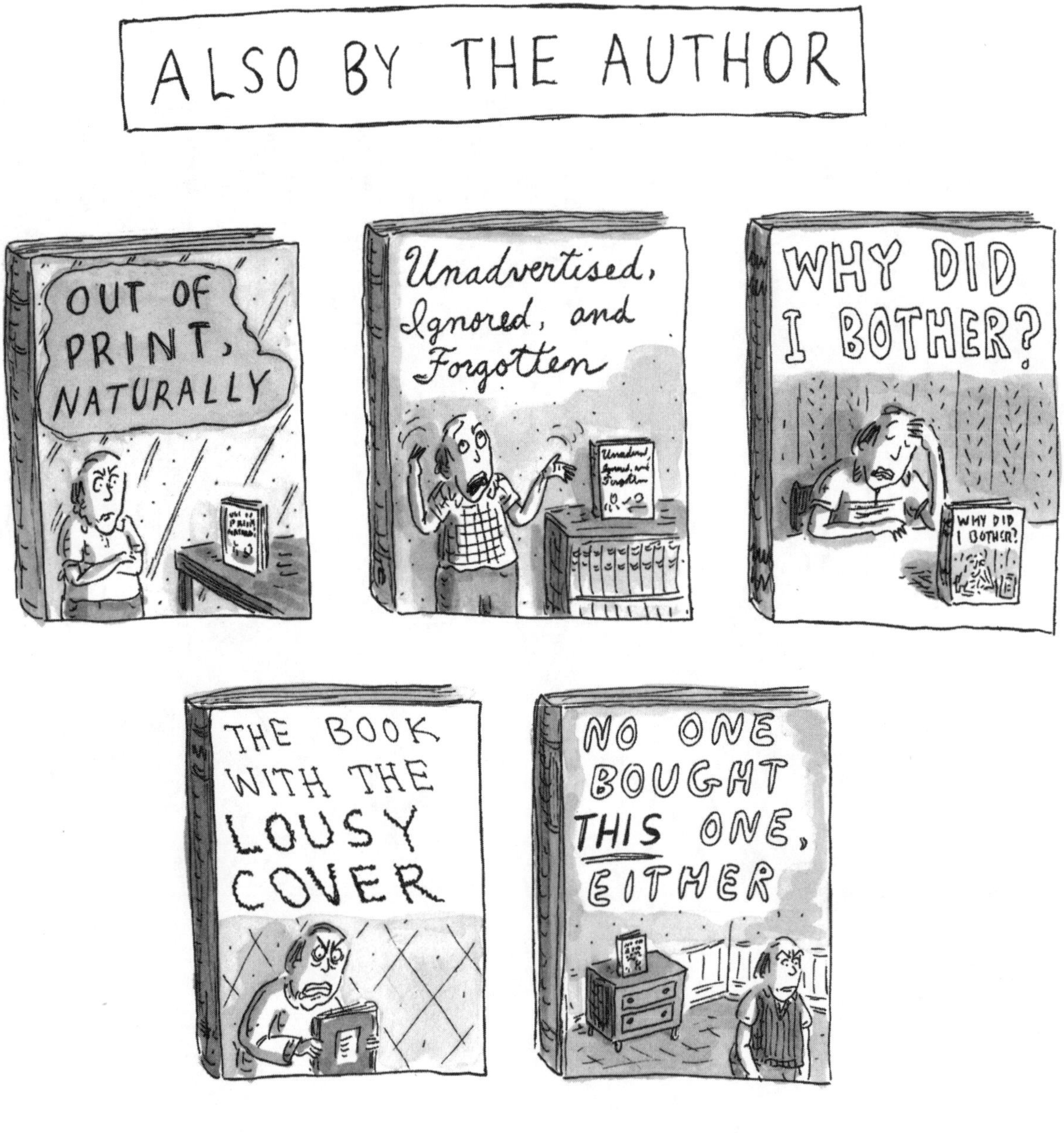
ALSO BY THE AUTHOR
OUT OF PRINT, NATURALLY
Unadvertised, Ignored, and Forgotten
WHY DID I BOTHER?
THE BOOK WITH THE LOUSY COVER
NO ONE BOUGHT THIS ONE, EITHER

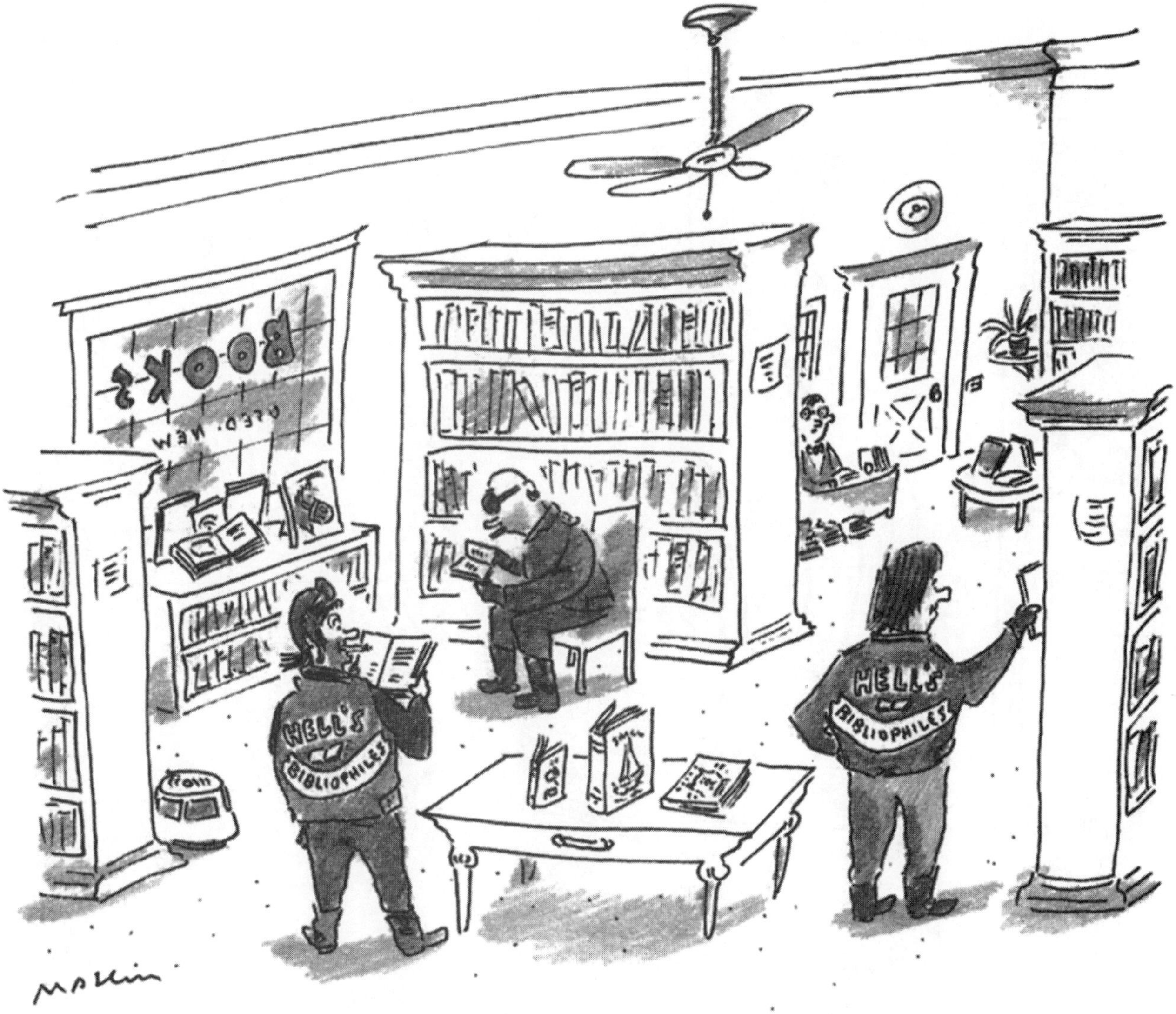
HELL'S
BIBLIOPHILES
HELL'S
BIBLIOPHILES

"*Congratulations! Your manuscript was the one-millionth personal memoir submitted to us this year.*"

"Susan Faludi would like to buy you a brewski."

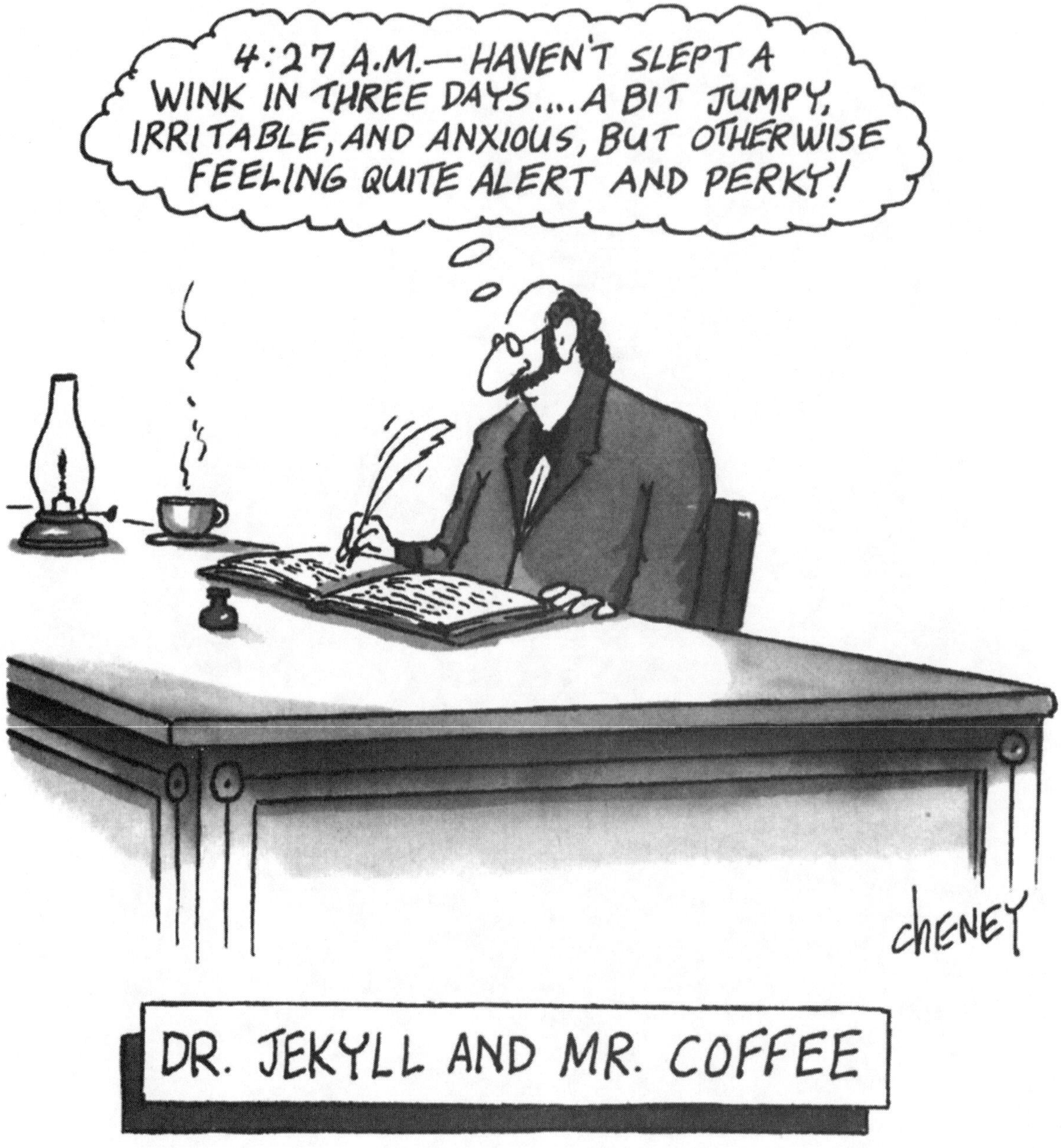
4:27 A.M.—HAVEN'T SLEPT A WINK IN THREE DAYS.... A BIT JUMPY, IRRITABLE, AND ANXIOUS, BUT OTHERWISE FEELING QUITE ALERT AND PERKY!
CHENEY

DR. JEKYLL AND MR. COFFEE

NET 'n' NOSH
(Formerly BOOKS 'n' JAVA)
M. Twohy

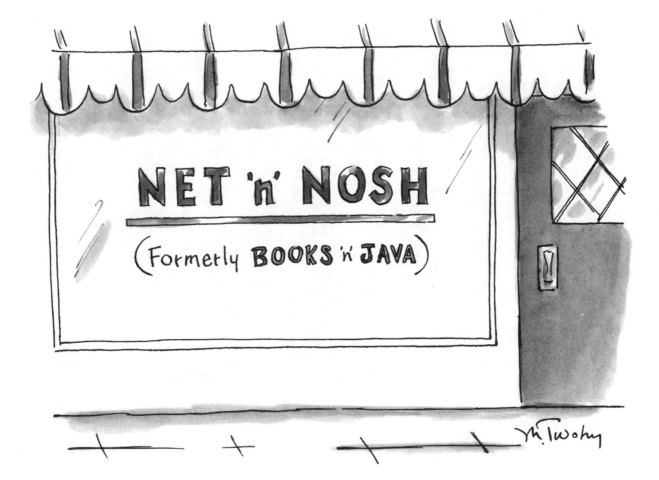

"You may well be from Mars, but the children and I are still from Westchester."

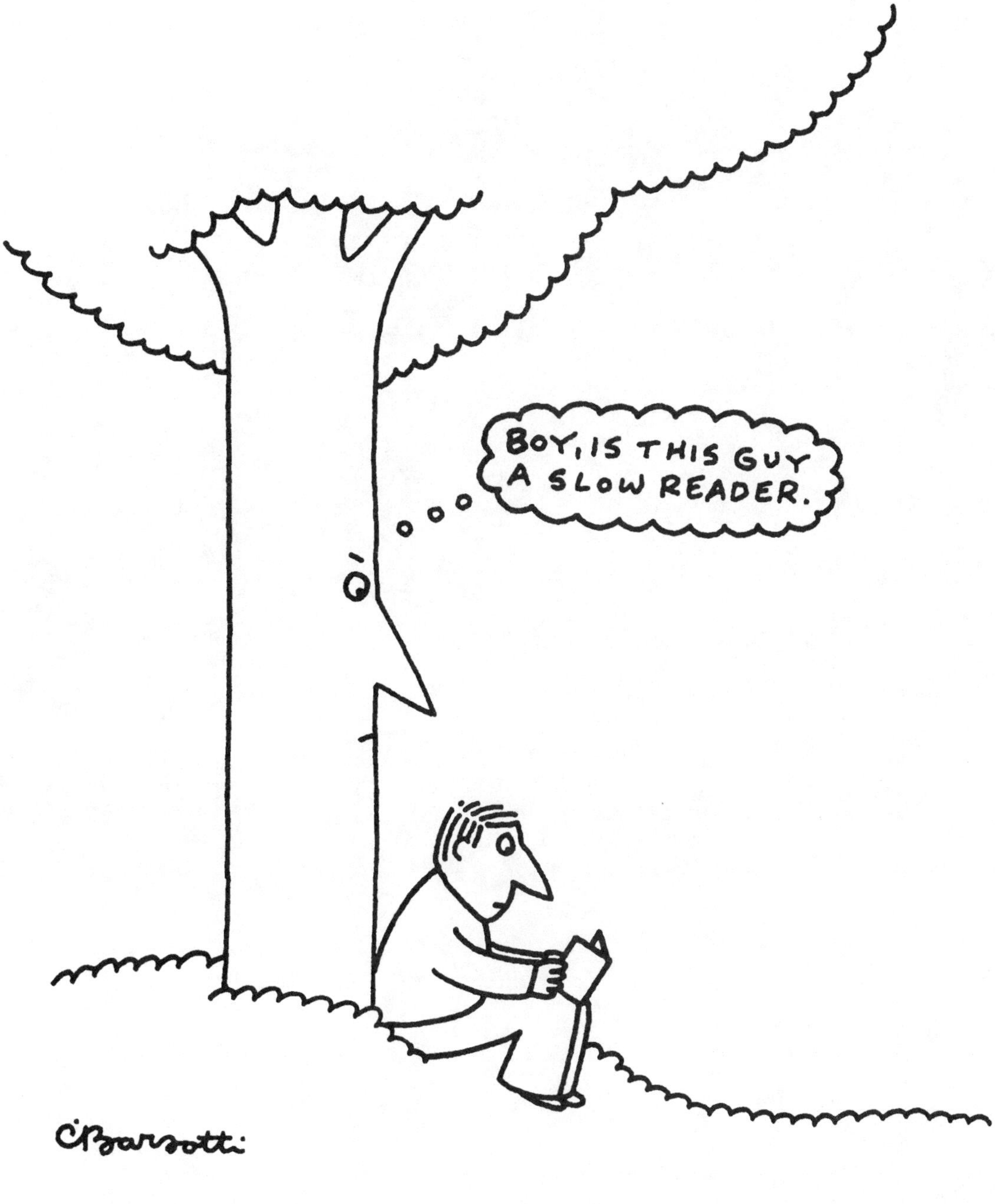
BOY, IS THIS GUY A SLOW READER.
CBarsotti

"Goodnight moon. Goodnight house. Goodnight breasts."

"In the novel based on my case, I'm acquitted."

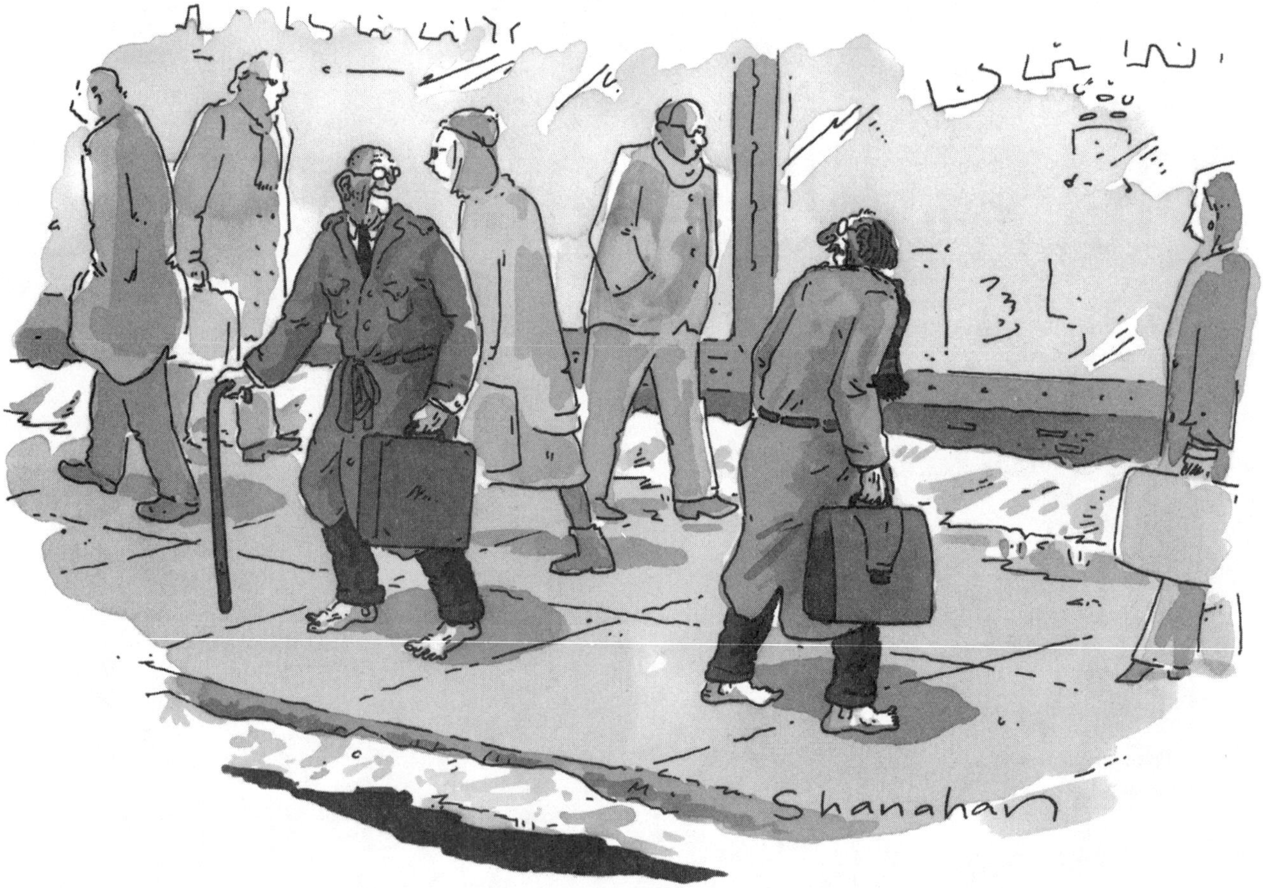
Shanahan

"It's me, Tom—Huck Finn!"

"What would you recommend to hold a seven-year-old girl's attention in a car from East Seventy-eighth Street to Bridgehampton?"

"Holy cow! What kind of crazy people used to live here anyway?"

"*Have ye seen a whale that matches this swatch?*"

"No, I don't think I have a book in me. I think I have a chicken in me."

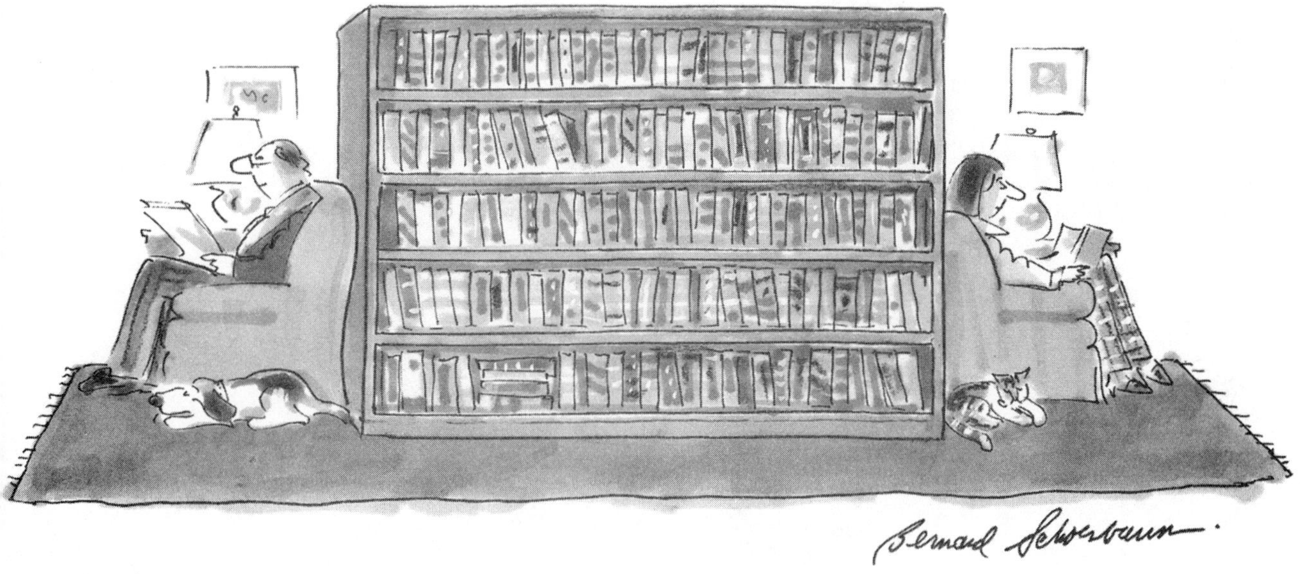
Bernard Schoenbaum

"I'm sorry, sir, but Dostoyevsky is not considered summer
reading. I'll have to ask you to come with me."

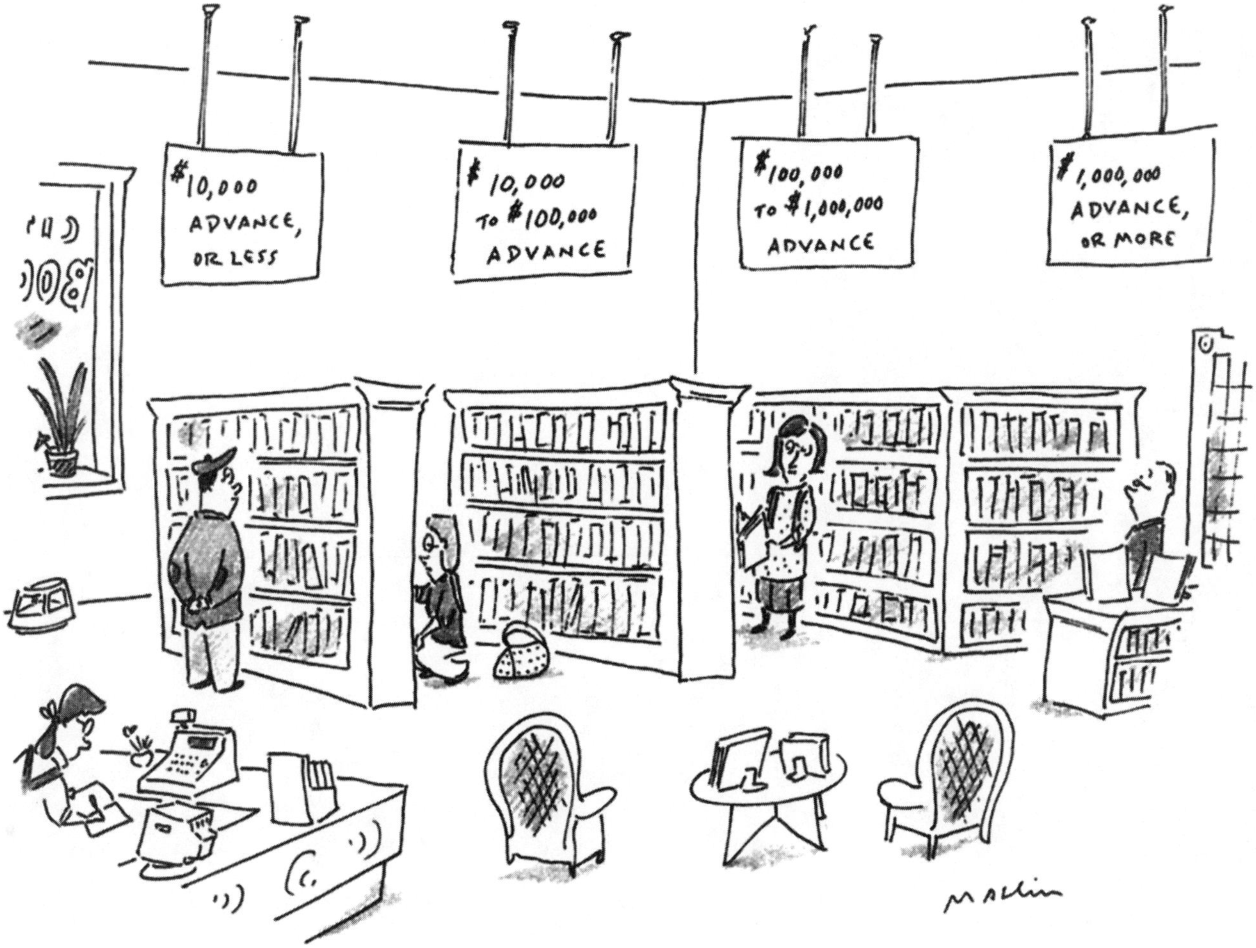
$10,000 ADVANCE, OR LESS
$10,000 TO $100,000 ADVANCE
$100,000 TO $1,000,000 ADVANCE
$1,000,000 ADVANCE, OR MORE
MAKIN

"Less roman, more clef."

Dickens' First Encounter with a Martini

DELUSIONS OF GRANDEUR

MANKOFF

"Get J. D. Salinger on the horn for me!"

"Are there any books that are still being
written for gentle reader?"

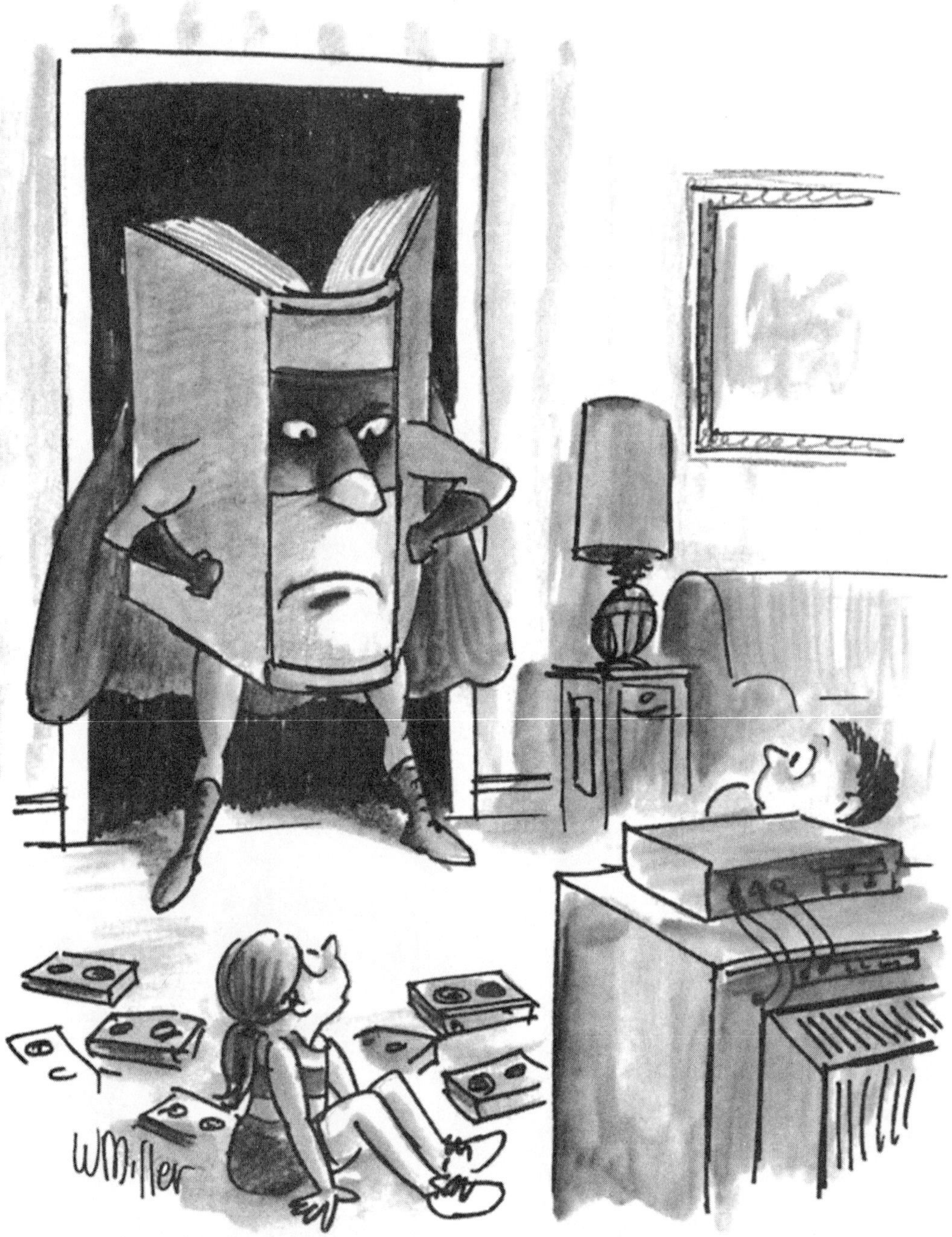
WMiller

ELOISE REVISITED

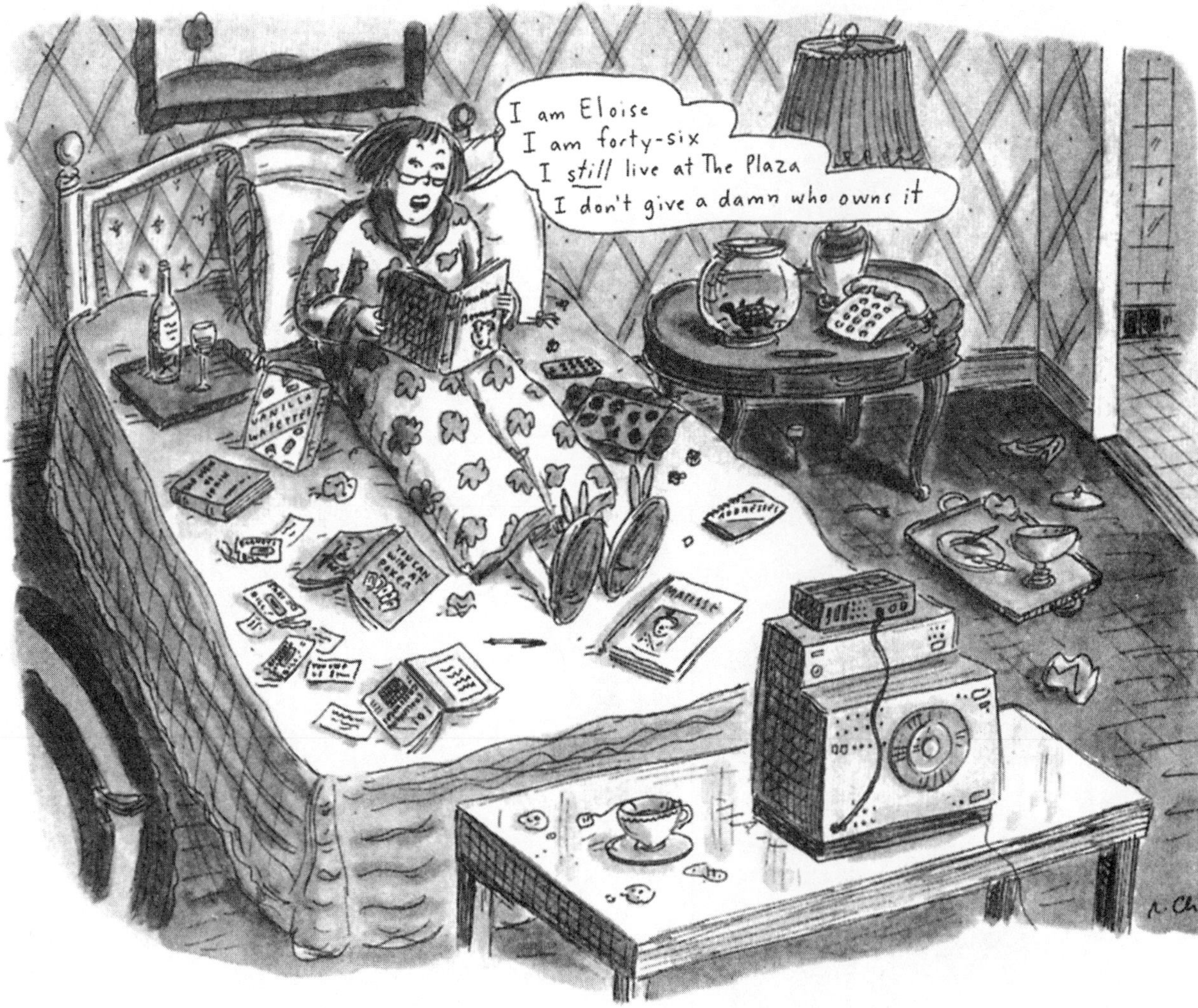
I am Eloise
I am forty-six
I still live at The Plaza
I don't give a damn who owns it

"I feel that I have at least one more unpublished novel in me."

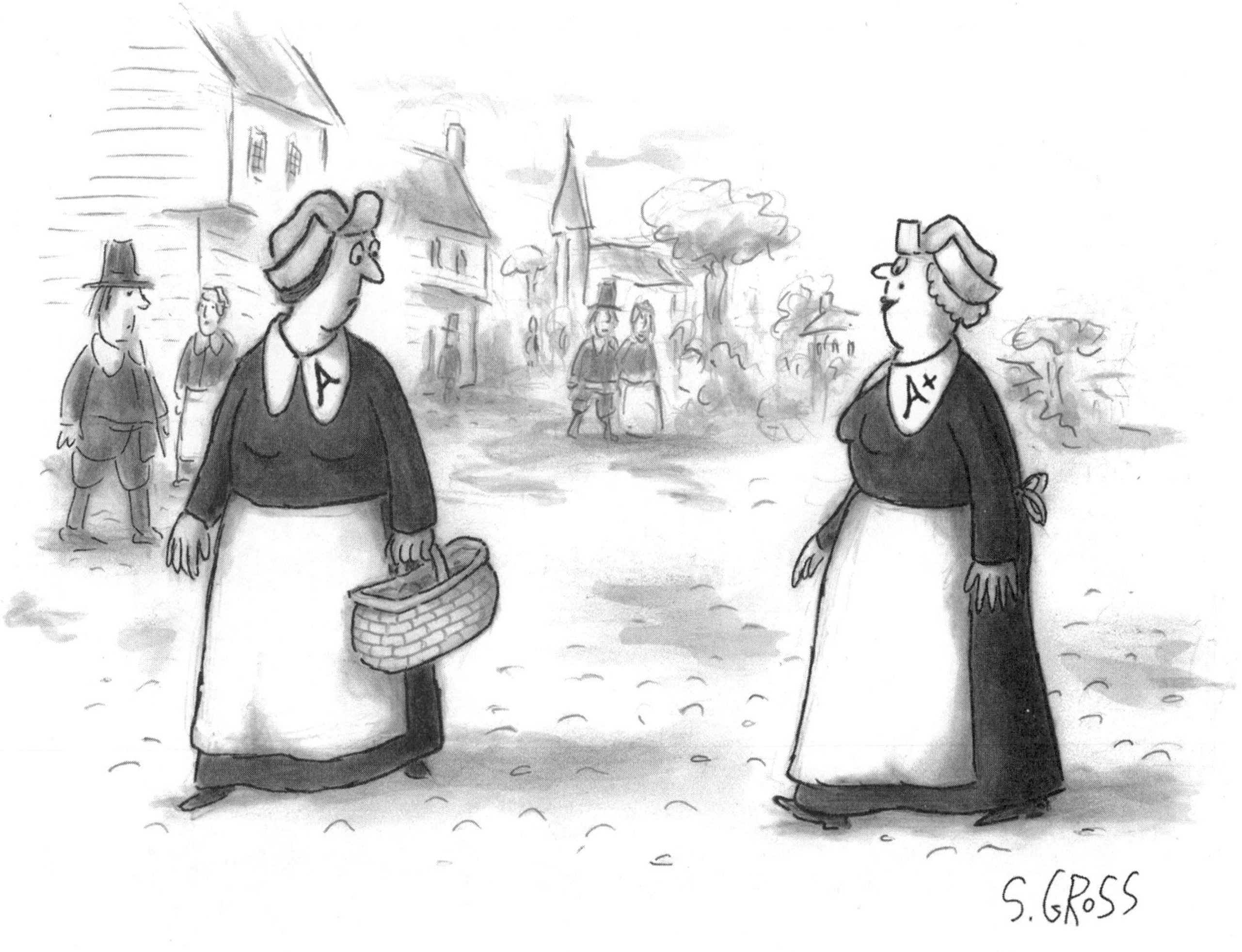
A
A+
S. GROSS

"Your book is a masterpiece, but, unfortunately, we're rather picky."

"Could you read the part where Stephen envisions life outside Dublin again?"

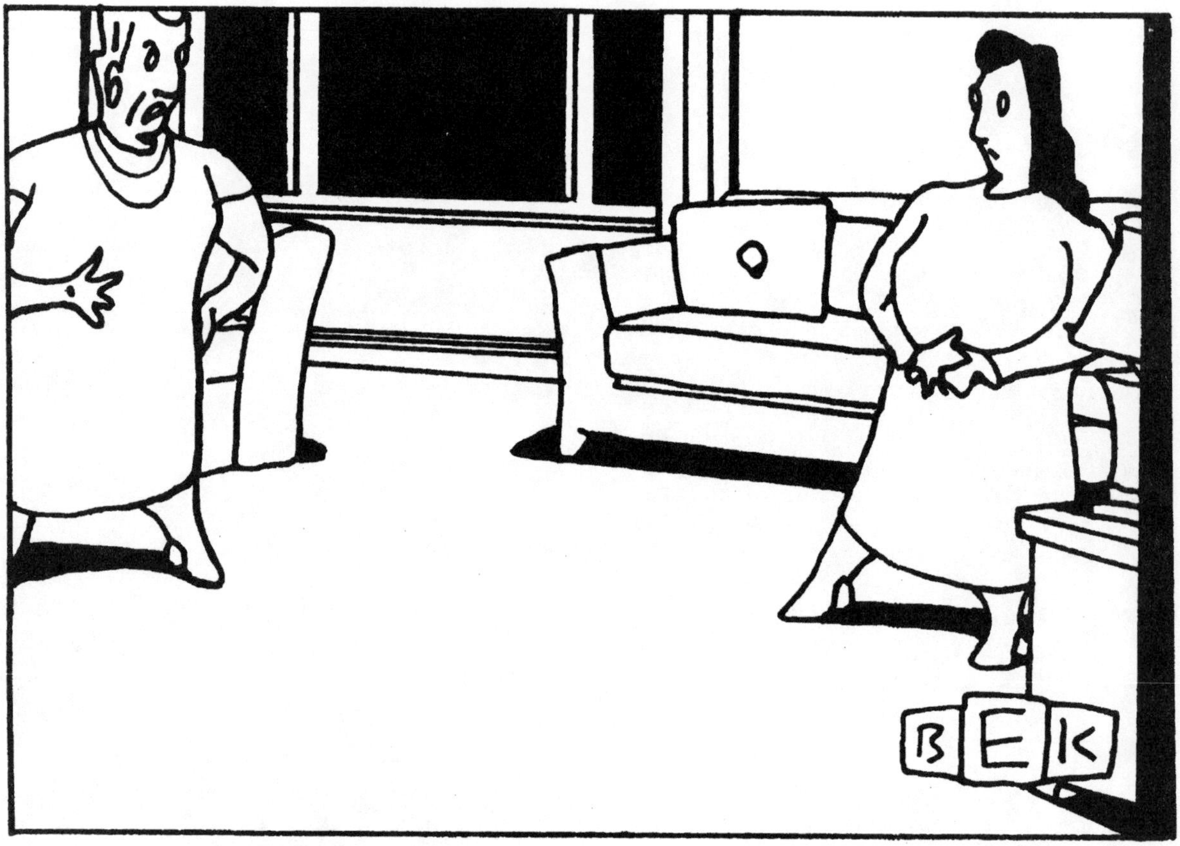
BEK

"What am I supposed to say when my friends ask why you're still a mid-list author?"

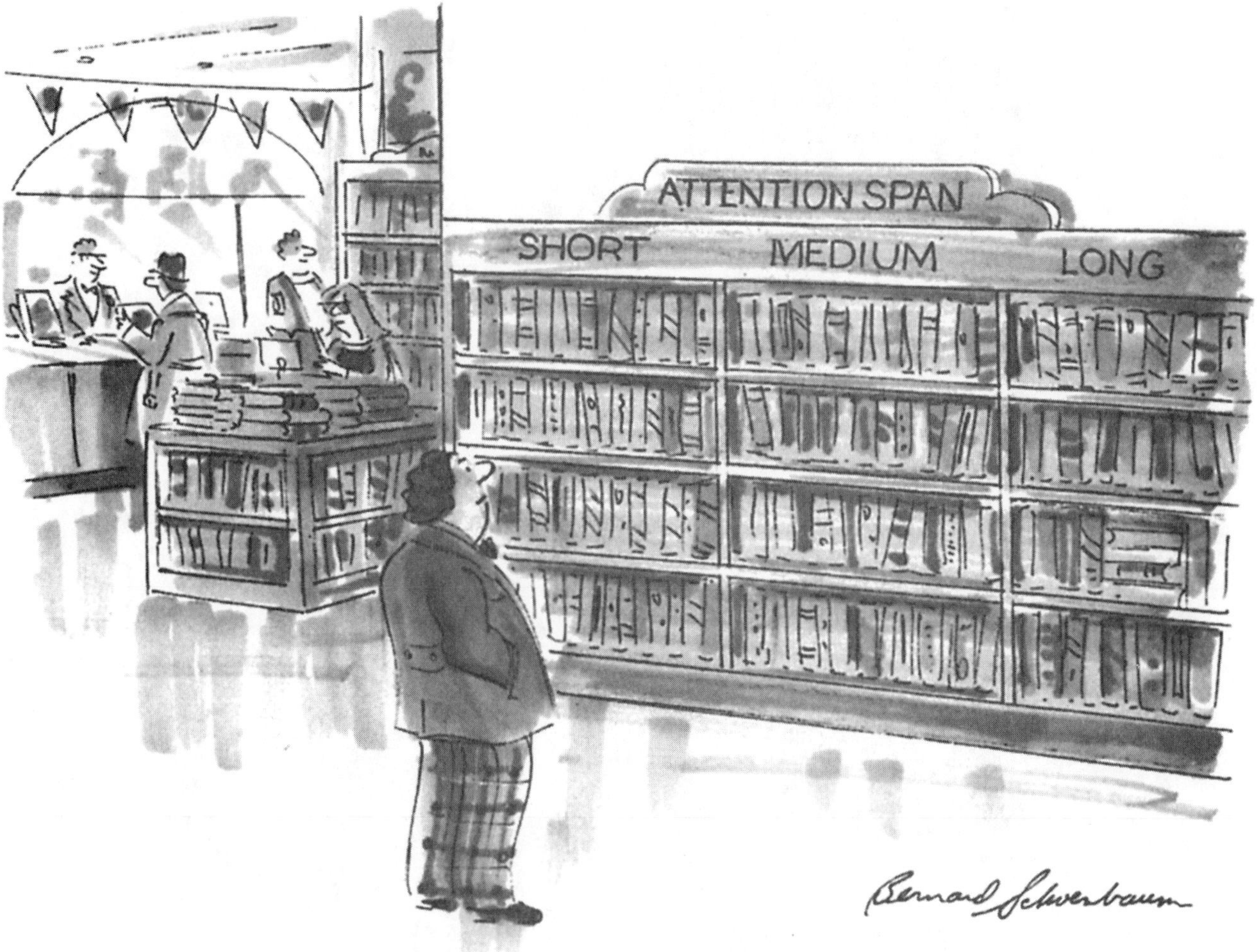
ATTENTION SPAN
SHORT
MEDIUM
LONG
Bernard Schoenbaum

"At last! A cinematic version of Twain's classic tale that truly represents our generation's ethos."

"Could you write, 'To Penny, my darling ex-wife, who
nurtured me and supported me all through my struggles as a fledgling
writer, and whom I blew off the minute I had my first big success.'"

NANCY DREW MYSTERIES

THE LATER YEARS

NANCY DREW
AND
THE MISSING HOUSE KEYS

I know I left them RIGHT THERE.

NANCY DREW
AND
THE MYSTERY OF
THE EIGHT POUNDS

How did I gain eight pounds? I eat nothing!

NANCY DREW
AND
THE SECRET OF
THE COMPUTER.

You and I are going to be GREAT FRIENDS!

R.Chw

"The Bible . . . that would be under self-help."

"*Words on paper, Ted. Just give us words on paper.
Our advertising people will do the rest.*"

"Sorry, Barrington, but you've failed to live up
to the glib promise of your early chapters."

"I'd like to buy this book and also the movie rights."

"The Icarus story is just that—a story."

"It doesn't work as a novel. But we're willing to publish it as a desk calendar."

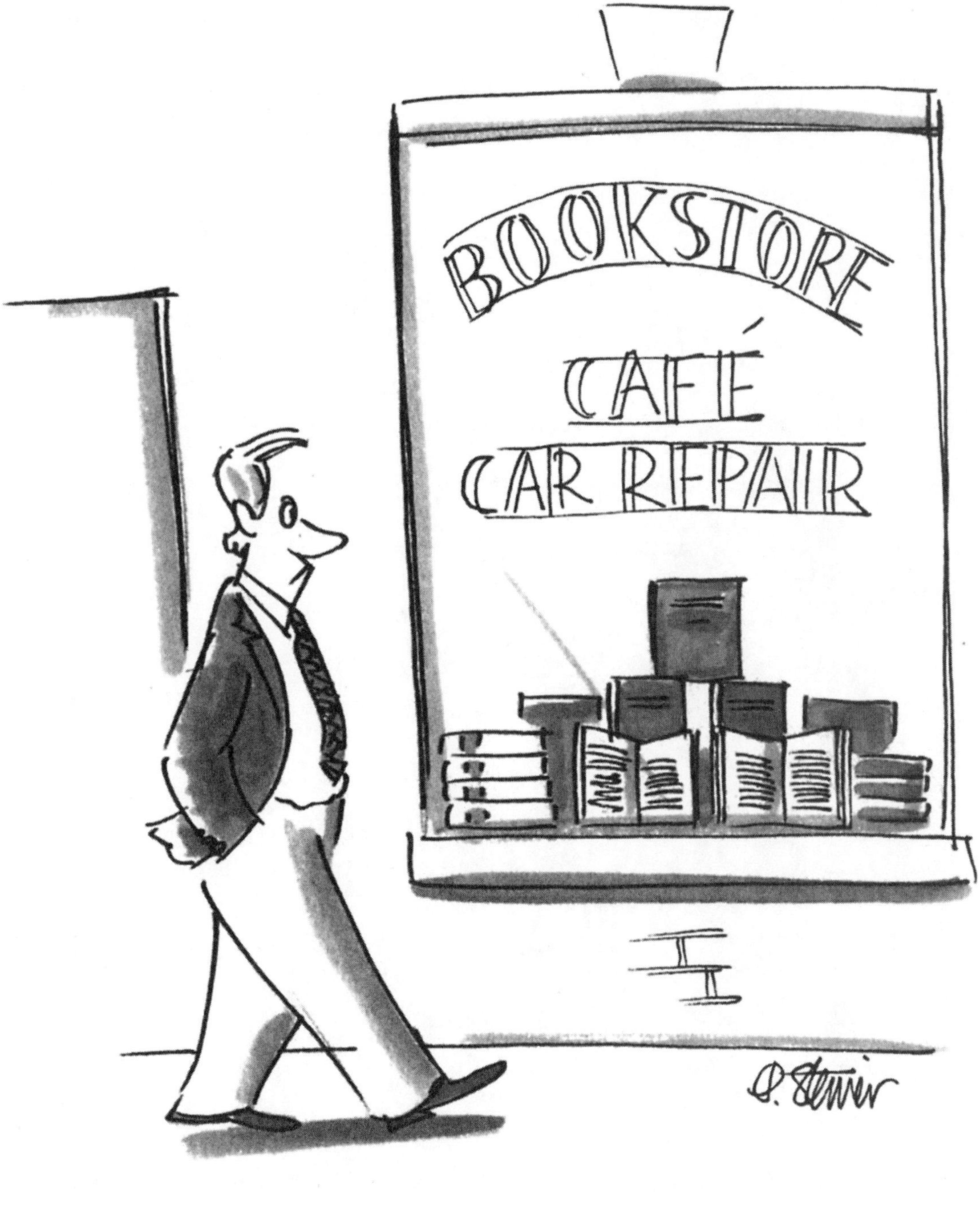
BOOKSTORE
CAFÉ
CAR REPAIR

"Your book nauseated me. Did you do that on purpose?"

"I'm afraid it's very close to something we've already turned down."

T.S. ELIOT MEETS BEAVIS AND BUTT-HEAD

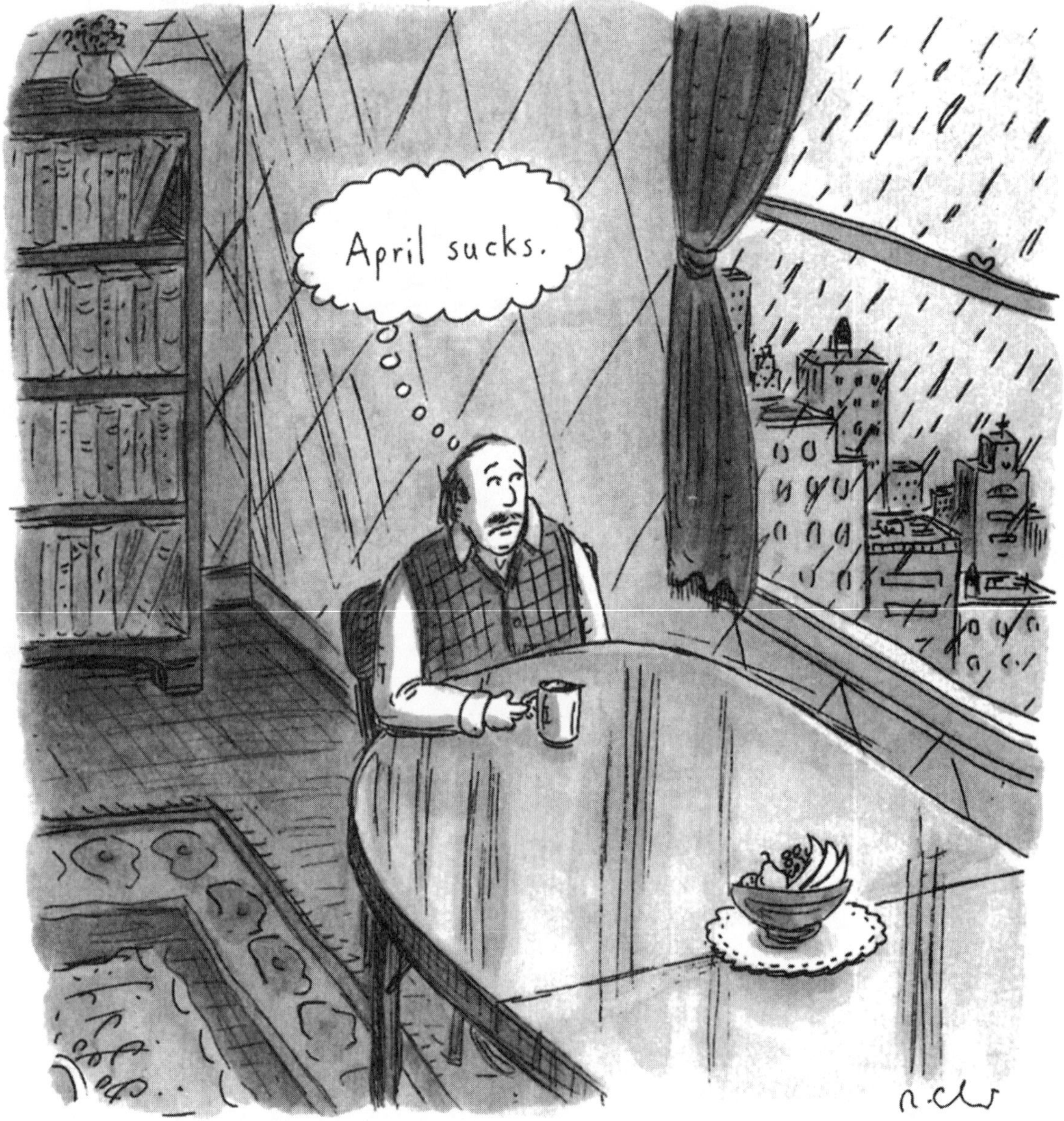
April sucks.

"'Chicken Vindaloo for the Hindu Soul' is but the tip of the iceberg in our initial strategy of global expansion."

"We have a calendar based on the book, stationery based on the book, an audio tape of the book, and a videotape of the movie based on the book, but we don't have the book."

INDEX OF ARTISTS